ALL
THEY
WANT
IS THE
TRUTH

The Challenge of Literature
Evangelism in Our Time

ALL
THEY
WANT
IS THE

ALL
THEY
WANT
IS THE
TRUTH

By
Bob Hoskins

*For your **FREE** copy of this book please write to:*

Book of Hope International
3111 SW 10th Street
Pompano, FL 33069
1(800) 448-2425
E-mail: info@bookofhope.net
Website: www.hopenet.net

OTHER BOOKS BY BOB HOSKINS

"Under the Guns in Beirut"
"The Middle East and the Third World War"
"The World's Greatest Need"
"Winning the Race for Russia"
"Russia: The Miracle of the Open Door"
"Study War No More"
"When Will Jesus Come"

ISBN 1-890525-30-8

© 1985 by Bob Hoskins. Printed in the United States of America. Published by *Book of Hope International*, 3111 SW 10th Street, Pompano, FL 33069.

Revised version © 2001 by Bob Hoskins.

Special thanks to Juanita Blackburn

Cover & Interior Design by George Hoskins

PUBLISHER'S FOREWORD

Bob Hoskins' ministry began the moment God gave him a vision at the age of seven. In that vision he saw an open Bible on a pulpit . . . and before him a multitude of seeking people stretching into infinity. That vision has compelled the founder of *Book of Hope International* to use every means available to reach the billions all over the world who have never had an opportunity to respond to the life-giving message of God's Word.

As you read Bob's story and catch with him a vision of the importance of Christian literature to combat the evils of this present day, we trust your heart will be stirred to have a personal involvement in getting God's message into the hands of people who otherwise have no hope for eternal life. What we do NOW will make a difference in their lives!

In 1987, God led Bob Hoskins and his team to launch the ministry of the *Book of Hope* for the children of El Salvador. This easy-to-read children's Scripture book was soon in demand for school children around the world. As of June 2001, some 143 million children worldwide have received the gospel in the *Book of Hope*. Statistics show that if each book is read by 4 to 8 people, more than 750 million people have read the Good News in their language. As God continues to bless, we can reach an entire generation of children all around the world!

All of us at *Book of Hope* are committed to reaching our world for Jesus. Each person's story is different, but God has led each one of us step by step to this place of worldwide ministry. It is an awesome but thrilling task, and we undertake it with the same vision that has inspired Bob Hoskins' lifelong ministry: a vision of hungry hearts in every tribe and nation searching for the TRUTH. We have the TRUTH, and we are determined that they shall have it too!

DEDICATION

This story could never have been written had it not been for a dear, wonderful man whose life and love for God have had a major influence on my own life and ministry. He is the man who believed with me that God had called me at an early age to preach the gospel, and he had the faith to help me launch forward as directed by God. From age 31 to age 38, which are sometimes the most productive years in a man's career, he laid aside his own dreams and ambitions and devoted himself wholeheartedly to helping me fulfill my ministry. He set up and managed my crusades nationwide, traveled with me, fasted and prayed with me, and was always there to give me his wise counsel. In his Spirit-given wisdom, he protected me from the promoters and opportunists who wanted to commercialize a boy preacher, rejecting lucrative offers in order to keep my ministry moving in accordance with God's revealed plan. Then, wisely determining that I was ready, at age 16, to go forward on my own, he let me go with his blessing. It is to this wonderful, wise, generous man that I lovingly dedicate this book:

To my Dad,
CHARLES H. HOSKINS

ALL MY LOVE
TO MY WIFE, HAZEL

Apart from my Lord and Savior Jesus Christ, my greatest debt of gratitude is due the beautiful, intelligent, personable lady that God gifted to me as my wife, Hazel. She was willing to leave only days after our marriage for a very trying and difficult mission trip to the remote areas of Africa, where her first house as a new bride was a thatched-roof hut with a cow dung floor. She was a faithful and contributing partner through our years of missionary evangelism around the world.

After the birth of our sons and our move to Lebanon, she was a stabilizing factor in those tumultuous years. She stayed bravely on even after having received numerous threats against her life, until she was sure, with me, that God was leading us somewhere else.

She has been the faithful mother who has poured herself into the raising of our three wonderful children. She has been the loving wife who has brought me more joy than I can ever describe. She has been the faithful servant of our Lord who to this day continues to give herself in ministry to others. There are no words with which I can adequately thank Hazel, but I want everyone who reads these words to know that without her love and her support, none of the ministry which I describe in these pages could have been possible.

Bob Hoskins

TABLE OF CONTENTS

Chapter I

TO
TELL
THE
TRUTH

*"To this end was I born, and for this cause came I into the world, that I should bear witness unto the **truth.**"*

John 18:37

> **B**ut these are **written** that ye might believe that Jesus is the Christ, the Son of God: and that believing ye might have life through his name.
>
> *John the Beloved*

1
SEVEN-YEAR-OLD PREACHER

"But, Dad! Jesus told me I should preach *now*!" I sobbed softly, standing before my father whom I loved dearly.

"Son," Charles Hoskins responded, placing his hand on my shoulder, "your mother and I prayed before your birth that God would give us a son - a son who would preach His Word. We believe God has answered our prayers. We sincerely believe you *will* be a preacher, someday, but not now."

Someday! Not now! The disappointing words echoed in my ears as my father continued.

"No seven-year-old boy can be a preacher, son. When you grow up, finish high school, and go to college, then you will be a preacher. That is what Jesus meant. He didn't mean that you should preach now."

My father had spoken to me with love and compassion, and I would never presume to tell him he was wrong. But I knew what Jesus had said to me. Even though I was only seven-years-old, Jesus' words to me had been clear and to the point: "Preach my Word!" And there was no doubt in my mind - I was to begin now.

Two nights earlier, following the service in our

local church, I had knelt at the altar and asked God to fill me with His Holy Spirit. I was filled - and more! I entered into a dynamic spiritual experience that continued for nearly six hours. In this experience my spirit left my body and Christ appeared to me, taking me on a "tour" of things past and things to come.

I sensed that I was hovering above my body, which was prostrate before the altar. In an instant I was looking at the glowing skyline of a city. I trembled with anticipation, for I knew this was heaven, the place of God's presence. Suddenly Christ appeared to me, standing perhaps eight to ten feet away. His physical body was somewhat obscured by a brilliant glow of whiteness or light surrounding Him. I cannot recall any physical features except His eyes. There was a powerful attraction: my eyes were fastened in contact with His, and I could discern His tremendous compassion and love reaching out to me. I also was aware that He saw everything there was to see and perceived everything there was to know about me. He said to me, "Bobbie, I want you to preach. Go tell people I love them and I have prepared a wonderful, eternal home for them."

Like all seven-year-old children, I had dreams of what I wanted to be when I became an adult. I was fascinated with airplanes, and at seven my dream was to be an acrobatic and test pilot. I told the Lord, "I am sorry, Jesus, I can't be a preacher, because I am going to be a test pilot when I grow up." I shall never forget the look on the Master's face at my refusal. It was one of disappointment and deep hurt, as if I had somehow physically struck or wounded Him.

In the next moment I had the same sensation I had experienced the first time. I was being whisked from my body, only this time, Christ and I were moving together. When the sensation ceased, we were on a broad street that was jammed with masses of people. And finally I stood with Christ on a great precipice looking into a sea of faces - men and women eternally lost, eternally damned. Even if I should try, human words could not describe the anguish and hopelessness I witnessed. Jesus said, "Would you, then, go warn them of hell and judgment to come?" Falling at His feet I said, "Jesus, I am only a seven-year-old boy. What could I say? What could I do?" Jesus said, "Bobbie, if you will only go, I will go with you. I will show you what you must do, I will tell you what you must say." Then I said, "Jesus, if you go with me, I will go and do all I can to warn men and women and to tell them of your love."

At that juncture, I felt once again that I was traveling, and I soon found myself standing before a pulpit. Upon that pulpit was an open Bible trimmed with gold. It was then that I clearly understood. It was God's Word, God's written, eternal Word, that stood as His warning to a lost world, offering the choice of heaven or hell, judgment or blessing, life or death! As my eyes lifted from the Book, I saw before me a multitude of people stretching farther than my eyes could see. There were people of all colors and cultures, and they were waiting for me to read from the Book and tell them of this eternal choice.

While I was still there, the Lord revealed to me that the first message I should preach was a message about His Second Coming. It was as if He said to me, and I perceived it mentally, "I am coming again." And not only should my first message be about the Second Coming, but I also had an awareness that there was a responsibility to tell men and women, as long as He gave me strength and breath to proclaim it, and that it is not a myth, it is not a figment of some excited imagination, but that Jesus Christ, the eternal Son of God, is really coming back to judge the living and dead. And the most important thing in the life of any man, woman, boy, or girl is to know and believe that He is coming and that they, by His grace and mercy, can be prepared for His return.

When I shared the details of this experience with my parents, their reaction was one of joy mixed with consternation. They did believe that during those hours when my body was lying prostrate at the altar something dramatic was happening in my life. But, the idea that their seven-year-old son was to begin preaching the gospel was difficult, to say the least, for them to accept.

For several days there was a kind of upheaval in our home. All I did was pray, cry, and plead with my parents to allow me, please, to obey Christ's command to preach. Finally, having no success in giving me rational arguments, my father took time off from his job to pray, fast, and seek God's guidance.

Shut away from everyone, Charles Hoskins prayed: "God, if You have told this child what he claims You've told him, and if he is to begin preaching now, as a child, then You must tell me also. I am responsible for him and I dare not let him begin doing the things he says You've called him to do unless You make it clear to me Yourself. I must be sure, for his sake, and for the gospel's sake."

For days my father sought God's wisdom. Through God's Holy Spirit, he was given to understand that what I had told him about my vision and call to the ministry was true. My father believed and accepted the fact that his seven-year-old son had seen Christ and heard Him say that he, Bob Hoskins, should begin preaching the Word. And from that time forward, I had my parents' full support in my ministry.

Within two weeks I preached my first sermon, the sermon Jesus had given to me. Then, through the power of God, more doors opened to me. Within a few years I was conducting city-wide revivals in auditoriums, tents, theaters, and other places - wherever God led us. Accompanied by private tutors, musicians, and my family, I toured the country from California to Florida preaching God's Word.

When I reached the age of sixteen, I began traveling alone. Then, two years later, at the age of eighteen, I felt the need to seek God's further direction for the future of my ministry. I felt a change was imminent, and I began to remember the things I had seen in my vision eleven years earlier. As I prayed for God's guidance, the Holy Spirit began to show me that I was to go into missionary evangelism. In fact, I was told the specific country where my overseas ministry was to start: *British Guyana.*

Speaking from personal experience, I should therefore say that if you want to open up a new area, the first thing to do is to send in someone with a Bible.

F. C. Glass,
Pioneer missionary

2
THE GREAT GUYANA
68-CENT CRUSADE

British Guyana! When these words came to my mind in prayer, I had no idea where British Guyana was located. I knew there were still many British colonies in Africa, so I began searching a map of Africa for British Guyana. Much later, I discovered the British colony on the northern coast of the continent of *South America*. I made some inquiries to learn if there were Assemblies of God missionaries there, and I found that there were none. I was perplexed as to how I, an evangelist, was to go there with no resident missionaries available to set up a crusade and be responsible for the follow-up.

I shared my problem with the pastor where I was conducting a crusade at that moment. As I explained what the Lord was saying to me, he got a startled look on his face. As it turned out, he was in contact with a small group of people in Guyana who had just recently received the experience of Acts 2:4. Within days, I wrote to the leader of that small group and told him how God had spoken to me. I asked if he would be willing to work with me in conducting an evangelistic crusade in the capital city of Georgetown.

I shall never forget his response. It was a strange mixture of positive and negative. He said that indeed they had been praying for revival in their nation and that they were excited about the possibility of my coming. They pledged themselves to cooperate and help in every way possible. However, he went on to explain that people in Guyana were very poor, and the small nucleus of Christians was not able to promise financial support. He made it clear that I would have to be responsible for financing the crusade.

After praying further about God's will and direction, I responded to his letter saying that I was grateful for their promise to work with me. I was enthusiastic about the spirit in which he had responded, and, as for the money, they should have no fears, for I would personally be responsible to finance the entire crusade.

When I wrote that letter, I was in the midwest United States. I had no financial reserves with which to buy a ticket to Guyana, much less finance a crusade when I got there. I did, however, have total assurance that God was speaking and that I must trust Him and step out in faith.

I called Pan American Airlines, making a reservation from Miami to Guyana, and asked them, prepare the ticket so that I could pick it up at the airport upon my arrival in Miami. When I made the reservation, I didn't even have enough funds to get to Miami. But the Lord supplied the funds as I made my way toward that city. When I reached Florida, I had almost enough money -

minus $20 and a few cents - to pay for my ticket.

I called a pastor in Miami, telling him I was on my way to this great overseas crusade. Fortunately, he invited me to spend the night in his home before the day of my departure. That evening as we sat at his kitchen table I explained how God had spoken to me. I emphasized that it was a step of faith, that I had no mission, no organization, in fact no single church sponsoring the crusade. I kept emphasizing that it was a step of faith, believing that he would feel something of my burden, catch something of my vision, and the Lord would use him to say, "Our church wants to be a part and we will give toward the crusade," and that he would provide at least enough to purchase the ticket.

Throughout the evening we talked and prayed. Yet, there was no indication that he or his church would become involved financially. The next morning at the breakfast table I went through the same exercise. In fact, I probably put a little more emphasis this time upon the fact that I was acting in faith. I did everything short of telling him that I really didn't have the money to pay for the ticket. Again he assured me of his interest and that he and his church would be praying. But there was no mention of any kind of material support.

The pastor was kind enough to drive me to the airport. When we got out of the car and stood by the open trunk, the moment of truth had arrived. All I had to do was to take my bag out of the trunk, walk into the airport terminal where Pan Am was holding my ticket, and pay for it. But there was still a shortage of funds. Once again, I said, "Brother, thank you. You will never know how I appreciate your interest, your hospitality, your kindness. As you know, as I have told you, this is a step of faith. Your provision of lodging and food has been such a blessing to me. I pray God will reward you abundantly." We stood there slapping one another on the back, and I was saying, "God bless you," and he was saying, "God bless you." After awhile it became a little ludicrous. There was nothing left to do except pick up my bag and go into the terminal.

Just as I reached the terminal door, I heard him call out, "Wait a minute, wait a minute." I almost tripped over my own feet getting back. He said, "I almost forgot. I wanted to give you this." He grasped my hand, pressing something into it. Could it be $100, $50, $20? I wasn't sure. What if it were only $10? I had this overwhelming urge to open my palm and look down. But that would have been impolite, standing there in front of the pastor.

However, as soon as I got inside the terminal, I looked. He had given me two bills, a twenty and a five. I had just enough money to pay for the ticket. When I boarded the plane I had $5.68 in my pocket.

When I arrived in Guyana, a small group, fewer than a dozen people, was there to meet me at the airport.

Almost before our greetings had been exchanged, the brother with whom I had been corresponding pulled me over to a corner. Now, I had told him in correspondence all that he should do. He should rent the largest auditorium available in the city. He should print 100,000 flyers and get them distributed across the city. He should reserve space in the newspaper for advertising. I also had suggested that he go to the radio station and try to buy time for a daily radio program. As soon as we were alone in a corner of the small terminal building, he reached into his pocket and unfurled this long paper where he had kept an accurate, detailed record of everything they had done, every cent they had spent. I could quickly see that not only had he been faithful to do everything I had asked, but also he had taken it upon himself to do a lot of things I had not requested. I quickly looked to the bottom right-hand corner, to discover that I was in debt thousands of dollars in a land where the average man's wage was about $12 per month.

I took the paper, folded it, stuck it in my coat pocket, and said, "Brother, you have done a tremendous job. I have never seen such a fine, detailed account." I later realized that had this dear, dear brother known I only had $5.68 in my pocket with which to meet those obligations, he very possibly would have had a heart attack on the spot.

The group took me to a hotel, which startled me

a little, because I had expected that at least someone would keep me in his home, which would save some expense. Yet, with every confidence that God had sent me, I checked into the hotel and signed the register just as if I had money to pay for my lodging. In fact, the next morning when I got up, I had breakfast, and again I signed the check with every confidence that God, who had spoken in such a powerful way, would supply through His own miraculous means.

It is a long and glorious story how, in the following weeks, God sent revival to the land of Guyana. The country at that time was going through a mini-revolution. The colonial government had clamped martial law on the nation. Initial permission for the crusade had been granted with a great many restrictions, one being that the meetings had to be held within the designated building only. From the first service, God had manifested His power in mighty miracles of healing. Blind eyes had been instantly opened. Some Hindu boys named Ramphal had brought their crippled mother. She had been confined for years to a wheelchair. By the time the service ended the city buses were no longer running, so she *walked* home with the boys, pushing the wheelchair before her. The entire family accepted Christ. The boys eventually were called into a full-time preaching ministry. When I visited Guyana about 27 years after that first crusade, one of those sons was the secretary-treasurer for the Assemblies of God in Guyana. His brother, Sidney Ramphal, came to the United States, where he has had a powerful ministry, particularly in the pioneering of churches in the inner-city communities.

By the third night of the crusade, miracles of healing had attracted such crowds that it became impossible for people to get inside the building. As a matter of fact, there were near riots as they clamored for entrance, beginning early in the afternoon. Some came early and waited the entire day just to get a good seat. A mass of people trying to get inside had been on wooden steps coming up one side of the building. The weight of so many had caused the stairs to collapse, fortunately without injury to anyone.

In a country under martial law, where the last thing the colonial government wanted was riots, I received an invitation to meet with the governor. In fact, the governor's limousine was sent to take us to the meeting. He asked my colleagues and me if we would move the crusade outside, at least to save the building from damage. This, of course, was what we had prayed for, so that there would be no limitations to the size of the audience. When we moved the crusade into the open air, crowds of approximately 30,000 people began to throng the grounds, again with many of them coming early in the afternoon to get a place near the front.

During those following weeks, thousands of

people made professions of faith in Christ as Savior. Multitudes received an infilling of the Holy Spirit. From night to night I explained to the people the joy of giving to the work of God. As we taught them the responsibility of stewardship that accompanies God's grace, they learned from the very moment of their conversion to start giving generously. As a result, when the crusade had concluded, every cent of the many thousands of dollars required for radio, auditoriums, advertising and other expenses had been covered.

A building fund was started with the aim of constructing a church to house these converts. They gave me a love offering which enabled me to travel throughout South America in countries I never thought I would visit, much less have the opportunity to preach in. When I arrived back in the United States, in Houston, Texas, I had one $5 bill in my pocket. The entire crusade and extended travel for meetings in other countries over a period of three and one-half months had cost me a total of 68 - cents!

I realized from that experience that God was indeed leading me into a ministry of missionary evangelism and that he would provide for my ministry.

Within months I was again traveling overseas, this time to the continent of Africa. In the thirteen months of my second missionary journey, God, by His grace, gave tremendous results throughout South and East Africa. Ours was the first open-air crusade ever conducted in the city of Dar es Salaam. Again, at the conclusion of the crusade, there was a congregation of more than 800 who had been converted and filled with the Spirit, to continue a witness in the city of Dar es Salaam and the country then known as Tanganyika, that was at the time under British colonialism.

Not long after I had returned from my first crusade in Guyana, God brought into my life a beautiful young lady, Hazel Crabtree. She was born a Canadian but raised in Bangor, Maine, where her father had pioneered and pastored for many years. We continued correspondence for five years as I traversed the world in evangelism. In September of 1959 we were united in marriage in Sacramento, California.

On March 11, 1960, six months after Hazel and I were married, we departed for Africa. Our first "home" was a mud house with a thatched roof. The conditions were not especially comfortable, but the Spirit of God was very real as we watched dozens, then hundreds, then thousands accept Christ and receive the baptism in the Holy Spirit. Our missionary endeavors took us throughout Africa and finally into the Far East. In April of 1963, after we had returned to the United States, our first son, David, was born. Following his birth we returned to South America and spent more than a year in evangelism work there.

During those years of extensive travel in many

countries, I was often reminded of the vision I received as a seven-year-old boy when God first called me to preach the message of redemption to lost men and women, boys and girls. As I looked into the faces of Africans, South Americans, Orientals, people from many tribes and races and nationalities, I saw again the necessity of giving them the living Word of God, which would make the difference between eternal life or eternal damnation for them. God continued to bless our ministry everywhere we went, and many thousands of people accepted Jesus Christ into their hearts and lives.

One thing that struck me deeply was that everywhere I traveled I saw widespread paganism - a lack of true knowledge and understanding about God, yet a fascination with spiritual things which was fed by brutal evil practices. But at the same time, as indicated by the response to my message, there was a deep, almost intuitive hunger for God's Spirit and His Word.

People all over the world recognized their need for something more - but most didn't know what that "more" was. In the sophisticated capitals of the world, the wealthy and powerful were always pursuing more wealth and greater power, but still they could not fill the gnawing void inside their hearts. In the jungles of Africa and South America, the uneducated and unreached people immersed themselves in superstition, witchcraft, and other evidences of paganism, yet they were never satisfied in their hearts - they found fear instead of peace.

Over and over, as I saw the multitudes, I said in my heart, "All they need is the Truth!" So everywhere I went, to everyone who would listen, I preached God's wonderful Truth of freedom, healing, and peace. and by the thousands they responded. They heard God's Word and knew this was the answer to the hunger they felt in their spirits. *He* was the answer they sought.

But what about those who didn't come to my meetings? What about the ones who never had the chance to hear my preaching, or anyone else's preaching? How would they - the untold millions - be reached with God's Truth? That was the question that constantly nagged at my soul for an answer.

Chapter II

THE
NEED
FOR
TRUTH

*"And ye shall know the **truth**, and the
truth shall make you free."*

John 8:32

It seemed good to me…to write.

Luke, the Physician

The Bible is the best missionary.

John R. Mott

3
A HOLY LAND
WITHOUT GOD

In 1964, the Lord impressed upon me that after 20 years of evangelism, I would soon move into a new type of ministry. With the urging of the Spirit to settle somewhere, Hazel and I began to pray for Divine leading. Through the past years, we had traveled into almost every area of the world in missionary evangelism. By the grace of God, we had witnessed great revivals that seemed to be sweeping through country after country. In Africa, South America and the Far East we had participated in these moves. At the time God was dealing with us in 1964, we were involved in tremendous meetings in the South Pacific.

One day, as I was praying, I placed before me a map of the world, asking God for direction. As I prayed, I traced with my finger the areas where revival fires already seemed to be burning. Then, as my fingers moved along the areas of revival, it struck me: right in the middle of the map was a gaping hole, an entire area of the world that was relatively untouched by God's Spirit. It was the *Middle East!*

I once came across a magazine article that dealt with the Middle East, and due to a typographical error, the title read, "The Muddle East." As I came to know the area, I wasn't so sure if that really was an error. There seems to be no end to the hatred and political intrigue that makes the Middle East a storm center of the world.

The nations that comprise the Middle East occupy some of the most strategic geography on our planet. It is there that three continents meet. It is the birthplace of the world's three leading religions: Judaism, Christianity, and Islam.

To many people it comes as a shock that this area of such importance historically, politically, geographically, and economically should for the most part be in spiritual darkness. Christians of all kinds - Orthodox, Catholic, and Protestant - comprise less than five percent of the total population. One study of world missions revealed that in 1964 there were fewer than 64,000 Protestant church members among the more than 100 million residents of the Middle East.

In the Middle East, more than anywhere else in the world, there is stark evidence of how the Church has lost its evangelistic initiative. After all, isn't the Middle East the "cradle of Christianity"? Isn't this where the Church began? We know the first disciples of Jesus did their part to spread the gospel. Everywhere you travel in the Middle East or Northern Africa you will see what are now mosques, but as the guides will point out, they were formerly Christian churches.

The early disciples blanketed the area faithfully

with the message of salvation. But as the Church became rich, politically acceptable, and even powerful, it lost its missionary fervor. And out of the Arabian desert came a new challenge to fill the void left by the Church with a brand new faith espoused by the "prophet" Mohammed.

The Arabs, filled with their newfound faith, swept out of the desert and conquered everything from Spain to China. And to assure that their faith would stand, they instituted laws and regulations against proselytizing by any religion other than Islam. Severe penalties were inflicted upon those who disobeyed. Economic and social pressures and physical intimidation were brought to bear against those who resisted Islam. Soon the gospel of Jesus Christ faded from the area.

For 1300 years - thirteen long, dark centuries - the Middle East has been virtually untouched by the gospel. At one time in Turkey, with a population of over 40 million people, there were only 50 known Christians. Only 50! And the same was true in the surrounding countries - few, if any, Christians could be found.

As I began to ponder the problem, my interest became a genuine burden for these masses who had been given little chance to accept or reject the claims of Christ. One of the problems was that in most countries, preachers were forbidden entrance, and it was even illegal for a person to embrace the Christian faith. In Lebanon alone, 150 years of Protestant missionary activity had reaped less than one percent of the country's population.

I made a full search of Scripture to find if perhaps this area was not prophetically included in what God had promised to do in the world. The more I searched, the more convinced I became that God's promises were to all people. Matthew 24:14 states, "And this gospel of the kingdom will be preached *in all the world* as a witness to all the nations, and then the end will come" (NKJV). Moreover, Joel 2:28 promises, "And it shall come to pass afterward that I will pour out My Spirit *on all flesh*" (NKJV).

Then as I read Acts 2:8-11, where the writer was describing the Day of Pentecost, I was impressed by the order in which the languages were listed: "And how is it that we hear, each in our own language in which we were born? Parthians and Medes and Elamites, those dwelling in Mesopotamia, Judea and Cappadocia, Pontus and Asia, Phyrgia and Pamphylia, Egypt and the parts of Libya adjoining Cyrene, visitors from Rome, both Jews and proselytes, Cretans *and Arabs* - we hear them speaking in our own tongues the wonderful works of God" (NKJV).

I wondered: Was it by accident that in this list the Arabs were the last to be mentioned? Could this be prophetic of a work of the Holy Spirit among the Muslim people which would be reserved for the end-time?

During this period of study and prayer, we received an unexpected telephone call from the Division of Foreign Missions of my church organization, asking if we would be interested in an appointment to work in the Middle East! Without divulging to them the things that had been happening in my own life relative to that area, I agreed to go to Beirut, Lebanon, and conduct an evangelistic crusade.

"A holy land inhabited by an unholy people," is the way one resident described this area of the world to me soon after my arrival in the Middle East. When I arrived in Beirut in December of 1964, it seemed to me that this city was the only logical point from which to begin. Beirut was the commercial and educational heart of the entire Arabic-speaking world. Its normal population of 750,000 was swollen by an influx of Arabs from other countries visiting on business or attending one of the city's universities. I saw Beirut as an island from which we could reach out and penetrate the areas that otherwise were closed to the gospel message.

Beirut was also the place where I would learn an important lesson. It was there, in the Middle East, that I would learn first-hand the real potential impact of gospel literature.

During our first crusade, unusual contacts opened a miraculous door of opportunity. We were granted permission to go on television from the city of Beirut with a one-year contract. From Beirut the telecast would potentially reach hundreds of thousands of people in five countries. By faith we accepted this opportunity and signed the agreement, obligating ourselves for tens of thousands of dollars. We did not have the money, and we did not know where we might get it.

Hazel and I decided to return to the United States to raise needed funds. Rev. J. Phillip Hogan, our missions director, suggested we call our mission "Middle East Outreach." For several months we traveled in the United States, presenting the challenge and opportunity of giving the gospel to the Arab world through television. Our days of itinerating were filled with miracles. In a remarkably short time, churches and individuals across the country responded and pledged support to our planned television ministry. In some services there were prophecies promising God's direction upon the Middle East Outreach ministries. Some told of visions they had seen of the gospel going out and reaching literally hundreds of thousands of people. Miraculously, the funds were given or pledged right on schedule. It was also during this period in the United States that our second son, Robert, was born.

Back in Beirut, in December of 1965 we began the work of producing the first telecasts to be broadcast. Then, without warning, only hours before we were to begin televising our programs, there was an upheaval in the government. Those who had been responsible for granting us the contract and permission to broadcast were removed from their offices. For six frustrating months, we negotiated at every level of the bureaucracy attempting to get the programs on the air, but to no avail.

It seemed our task would be even more difficult now. We moved our emphasis to a Center of Evangelism with a program of literature outreach. We knew rents were high and good facilities would be hard to locate. But soon we were led to an appropriate building, and as quickly as possible we prepared it for the launching of a crusade and the opening of the Center of Evangelism.

It was Sunday, September 11, 1966. This was the day of our opening. It hadn't rained in Beirut for five months, but today looked threatening. However, soon the clouds lifted and the sun shone gloriously.

The attendance at our inaugural service surpassed our expectations. By the scheduled time of the service, a near capacity crowd had gathered. Most of those present had never attended an evangelical church in their lives. Yet, they listened intently to the message preached, and following the service, many raised their hands, indicating a deep spiritual hunger.

After many months of frustrations and seeming setbacks, our Center of Evangelism was opened, and our ministry was begun in the key city to the Middle East: Beirut.

We still believed that Beirut was primarily to
be a base, an island, from which we could reach out to
larger areas. But how could we reach those areas and
their people? We knew preachers were not welcome in
most of the areas. We had tried to begin a television
ministry but had come against a brick wall. We knew
God had called us here to spread His Word, but how
were we to do it? I began to pray and search God's
Word for enlightenment.

The Bible reveals to us that even before God
sent His Son to die on the cross, the redemptive process
had begun. This is evidenced by the Old Testament sa-
crifices and the laws that God gave to His people. As I
read the Bible and prayed, something very significant
began to emerge in my understanding.

From the early days of recorded history through
to the end of the New Testament, almost every major
event on God's calendar in dealing with mankind was
preceded by and its impact was perpetuated *through
some form of written communication*! God "put it in
writing!"

Many of God's great men spoken of in the Bible
- His written Word - were writers. The prophets wrote.
The kings wrote. The apostles wrote. Many of Christ's
followers - physicians, lawyers, ministers, teachers -
wrote. And God, Himself, when He gave the Ten
Commandments to Moses, wrote with His finger on a

tablet of stone. Throughout our world's history, God has imparted and perpetuated His Truth, His law, His message through the written Word.

How could one man reach the lost of his generation? How could even a group of men or several groups of men evangelize *three billion* unreached souls with the Truth they needed?

I had my answer. They could be reached *through the written Word.* Where men could not go, the written Word could reach. Where one person could do little, the written Word could do much. It was there in the Middle East that I was to learn once and for all just how effective God's written Word could be in reaching the world with the Truth for when it so desperately longed.

Literature was the answer. Living in the Middle East, we had ascertained the tremendous respect that the Muslims had for anything printed. Islam is a religion of *the book*; of the more than 170 countries of the world that I have visited, I have found no people anywhere with a greater respect for printed materials than the Muslims have. So literature was the answer to reaching them with the Truth they were seeking.

But how would we get the literature to them? We thought of some rather unusual schemes to spread gospel literature throughout the Middle East! For example, we thought about flying over the cities and "bombing" them with thousands of gospel leaflets. This method would have been ridiculous in the Middle East, and we knew that we would probably never know if the leaflets were read. We had to spread the message in a way that would guarantee some kind of feedback. We needed to be able to offer a follow-up ministry to ensure that any new converts would have the opportunity to grow spiritually. But how would we manage this?

We devised a simple set of six lessons about the Bible and the redeeming power of Jesus. The lessons were written in a way to arouse curiosity, and hopefully lead people to respond by working through the entire series. By faith, I had thousands of these lessons printed.

Then we managed to buy small amounts of advertising space in a Beirut newspaper. We inserted an ad, offering these six simple lessons on the Christian faith. We had no idea what to expect in the way of a response - we would have been happy with just one!

Much to our amazement and excitement, we received responses from eight Arabic-speaking countries. In a few months, we had enrolled several thousand Arabs in our "correspondence school." Soon we had enrolled 10,000! 20,000! 50,000! 100,000! 200,000! 300,000! In less than ten years, more than 400,000 students from 26 Arabic-speaking countries were enrolled in our literature program.

Is it possible that in a country where there is no Church, and where it is illegal to embrace any religion other than Islam, someone can request and receive in the mail a gospel lesson, study in the privacy of his room, and be brought to know the saving power of Jesus Christ?

The answer is YES! A resounding and glorious YES!

The power of the gospel is not in a building. It is not in a man. The power of the gospel is in the gospel! The gospel is the power of God unto salvation! The Holy Spirit does not have a nationality - He embraces *all* nations! The Holy Spirit is not bound by men's laws and regulations. He doesn't need a passport. The Holy Spirit can go where He wills, and nothing and no one can stop His sovereign move among men. And we soon discovered that wherever we could get the Word of God in printed form, even without a preacher, the Holy Spirit would accompany the written Word, revealing Christ and bringing Muslims to a knowledge of saving *Truth*.

In every area where there is revival, we have found literature has paved the way. The Holy Spirit is doing the work through literature, and we are reaping the harvest.

A veteran missionary from Indonesia

4
THE POWER
OF PAPER AND INK

Why did we receive such a great response to our literature? What made these pieces of literature so valuable? Four reasons came to mind as we pondered this phenomenon:

First, much of the world was emerging from illiteracy into a newly-discovered literacy which created in people the desire to study. This was especially true in the Middle East, where the people would study Communism or the Bible, depending upon which type of material was available. In recent years, the drive for literacy has accelerated all across the globe. People everywhere will accept whatever kind of literature they can get - whether it is of God or of the devil!

Second, the printed page can be distributed through the government-operated postal system. In the Arab world, literature went where missionaries and national preachers could not visit.

Third, literature not only can reach, it can teach. Students learn step-by-step and are satisfied. Books, too, can promote steady spiritual growth when they are used as supplements to the Bible. Testimony and teaching books help to contemporize the Bible's message, and clarify difficult doctrines. They are, in a sense, "paper" pastors!

Fourth, tracts, books, and study courses all have the psychological advantage of promoting anticipation and expectation. Each one is like a continued story segment - "Don't miss the next thrilling episode!" And finishing a book, a course, or a series of lessons is like having climbed a mountain. It gives a sense of growth and attainment. Also, books provide a sense of ownership, making a person's faith more his own, as well as providing immediate access to a wealth of substantial helps. Books have been called "a university in print."

During the first year that we offered the "Way to Life" courses, 8,250 students enrolled. Of these, 1,616 completed the series and received graduation certificates. But even more thrilling are the testimonies that poured in. More than 1,000 students testified to receiving Christ as their personal Savior, and about 70 percent of those were Muslims!

One student wrote to us from Tripoli: "Thank you for your valuable studies. I can testify that I was converted and now have the heavenly life." Another, a Muslim, wrote from Egypt: "These lessons have brought light to my dark heart. I have learned Jesus loves me for He has forgiven my sins." And another student wrote, "I have studied my Way to Life course and I have realized that Jesus is more than just another prophet. He's the Savior of the world. I know it because He's now my Savior."

Within a short time we were receiving 50 testimonies - 100 testimonies - 200 testimonies - each month! During an eight-year period, we received an average of more than 500 authenticated testimonies every month from countries that had been considered completely closed to the gospel of Jesus Christ. The need for Christian literature was obvious - and so was its effectiveness.

Eventually we began publishing the *Way to Life* magazine and sending it to our students in the 22 countries with which we had contact. It was virtually an instant success.

It was my hope and expectation that these first students of the Way to Life School would form a nucleus of believers, and that these would be baptized in the Holy Spirit and begin reaching their nations for Christ. I looked forward to the day when the doors to some of these countries would open and somebody would be able to go in and hold evangelistic crusades.

I decided that, in light of this anticipation, we should begin teaching our students concerning the infilling of the Holy Spirit. We began to run a series of articles in *Way to Life* magazine concerning the Person and work of the Holy Spirit. I didn't expect anybody actually to be baptized in the Spirit merely from reading a few articles, especially since the subject was entirely new to their thinking. But rather, our hope was that readers would be alerted to the possibilities of further spiritual growth available to them through continued study of the Bible.

After only a few articles had run in the magazine, we received a rather unusual letter from one of our readers. He stated, "I have been reading in your magazine about this baptism of power. But the articles didn't say whether we *should* have this power, or even if we could have this power. But it seemed that some people, according to the articles, did have this power. So, since the articles didn't say, and I didn't know, I did what previous articles had told us to do when we needed an answer, and I prayed to God. I told God that I liked what I read about the power, and that if I should have it, and could have it, I'd like to have it. So, God, please give it to me."

What do you think happened? Of course, he got what he asked for! There was no doubt, based on the rest of his letter, that the man had been baptized with the power of the Holy Spirit - and he had received his baptism without the benefit of a church or even a preacher.

I was so excited reading this letter that I ran through our office waving the letter saying. "You'll never believe what kind of miracle has happened! It probably won't happen again in a hundred years!" But a few days later another letter arrived telling almost the identical story. Then another letter! And another! And yet another!

What was happening was beyond my wildest expectations - but that's the way God likes to work. Quickly, we produced a 16-lesson course on the Holy Spirit, and this time we included details about who could receive the power, and *how*. Every time we received a testimony of conversion, or baptism, we enrolled the writer in the course on the Holy Spirit. And again, over these years, in countries previously believed to be nearly impervious to evangelism, God was filling people with the Holy Spirit.

In Egypt, there are more than eight million Coptic Christians. The Coptics deny that the incarnate Christ was both fully man *and* fully God, but believe He was solely divine in nature. A Coptic priest enrolled in our course, and as a result was baptized in the Spirit. Consequently, he began preaching the gospel message to his congregation of more than 600 people. Within six months, 300 people in that Coptic church had been baptized in the Holy Spirit. The situation so upset the church hierarchy, based in Cairo, that it was decided the priest had to be moved. At first the Coptic leaders attempted to get him out of the country by enticing him to go to America to study for his doctorate, but he refused. Then they decided to move their rebel pentecostal priest to an obscure parish where they thought he would quiet down. But they were wrong. He preached the gospel message to that church, and then there were two pentecostal Coptic churches in Egypt! And since that time, it has been estimated that there are probably more than 500,000 Spirit-filled Coptics in Egypt.

To be ostracized, criticized, and perhaps to die for an expression of faith in Someone with whom one is not really acquainted is what the Church had been asking Muslims to do for decades. Showing an interest in the Christian faith, even to the extent of entering a church, would bring upon a person suspicion and even death in many parts of the Arab world. It was no wonder the Church had made so little progress in leading Muslims to Christ.

The congregation of the Middle East Outreach was the entire Arabic-speaking world. We did not ask them to jeopardize their lives by entering a building. We did not ask them to stand and testify to a faith in Someone they did not yet fully know. Instead, we sent to them the Good News of salvation, in the privacy and protection of their homes. In the seclusion of their inner rooms, they could read, study and be led by our literature to knowledge of Jesus Christ. When we looked at our files, thinking of the thousands upon thousands of names recorded there, we envisioned that great group as our congregation.

Week by week, through the courses and the supplemental literature we sent them, we were leading our students to a relationship with Christ. Books, tracts, and often personal letters guided them to a knowledge of the Master. We asked them for a response by giving them an opportunity to do something, such as a crossword puzzle, or to enter a contest in our *Way to Life* magazine. Thousands answered.

I was thrilled to see hundreds of thousands of names and addresses in rooms filled with files, and I was excited to read their testimonies. But I am orthodox enough that I wanted to see some of these believers. In 1968 with a colleague, I set out to visit some of our students in the land of Iraq. The Middle East was still suffering the aftershocks of the 1967 Arab-Israeli war. Iraq still considered itself to be at war not only with Israel but also with America. Our visit there was a disaster. We were seized by the Iraqi authorities and accused of being agents for the CIA. We were dragged off to one of their wretched prisons where we underwent days of intensive interrogation, and only by God's grace were we delivered.

(I mean *delivered*: six weeks after we escaped the country, 13 people were hung in the city square of Baghdad - people who had been arrested at the same time as we, and accused of the same crime.)

When I returned to what was then the relative safety of Beirut, I did a lot of heart-searching and reading again the words of Jesus in Matthew 16:18, *"I will build my church."* I realized that my American presence was probably a barrier to the spread of the Gospel in lands like Iraq. Yet I knew that if the church was going to truly be planted and expand, they needed trained leadership. The mission of the Church is to plant churches.

My next idea was that we should start a Bible school, training students from all these Muslim countries and sending them home to evangelize their own nations. Some of the people with whom I shared the dream were not nearly so excited. In fact, one man said, "It's crazy to put a school here for people who will never be able to get here." The strained political situation throughout the Middle East and the sporadic fighting among the various countries made it almost impossible for citizens from one country to travel freely to another. For many of the same reasons I could not go to my correspondence students, they could not come to me. But the dream had become so real that my response was:

"We'll build the school, and God will call people out of these lands, and they will come here if they have to crawl through barbed wire fence to get here."

I wasn't sure at that moment if those words were from God or if they were Bob Hoskins' enthusiasm for the dream. Through the years, however, I found that it was nearly a prophetic statement, for most of the students who came to our Middle East Evangelical Seminary came under impossible circumstances.

Let me tell you about two young men from the country of Iraq. They came to Christ through our literature ministry. They received a knowledge of the Holy Spirit and a spiritual baptism through our literature. They read in our student magazine about the Middle East Evangelical Theological School and felt that it was God's will for them to attend the school, but that was impossible. Their country was at war; they were military age; they could not obtain passports. If they had passports, they wouldn't be given visas to leave the country. But these young men, after fasting and praying, set out on a very bold - although it seemed ridiculous - journey.

They went straight to the capital, Baghdad, to the Ministry of the Exterior to ask for passports and visas! All human rationale said, "impossible, absolutely insane." They barged into the outer office of the ministry, and told the secretary that they had come to see the minister. The secretary said, "That's impossible. His appointments are scheduled months in advance. You can't see him."

Finally, after they had asked several times, the exasperated secretary, simply to humor them and hoping to be rid of them, asked, "If I ask the Minister to see you, and he says he will not, do you promise that you will leave?" They said they would. When the secretary returned, he said, "I apologize. I have the Minister's calendar, I know of all his appointments. I have never seen your names. I have never heard of you, but he says that not only does he know you, but that he is expecting you."

One of the young men later told me, "When the secretary said that, my hair almost stood on end. We had not told anyone we were coming except our parents, and they were hundreds of miles away."

When they entered the minister's office, he stood and greeted them by name. He said, "I've started filling out your papers. I have to ask you a few more questions, then I'll sign and you can give these to my secretary. He'll take care of everything." He asked the questions and signed the papers, then began to usher the boys out.

"Excuse me," one of the young men asked, "we're puzzled. How did you know our names and what we wanted?"

He said, "How did I know? You certainly know better than I. There was a man in my office not 15 minutes before you arrived. He was the one who told me who you were and what you wanted, and what I should do for you. What do you mean, how do I know what you wanted?"

When they arrived in Beirut for Bible school, the young men reported, "We knew God had sent an angel into that room who had prepared the mind of this Muslim minister to give us our travel documents."

Three years later, they graduated from Bible school and returned to Iraq to do what I had hoped to do years before. Today in Iraq, there are scores of bodies of believers where these young men have gone into towns and villages, contacted those who were led to Christ through our literature, and brought them together as fellowshipping bodies of believers.

When the Holy Spirit makes Christ real to people, we have ample evidence that they are then willing to take a stand and make an open confession of Christ as their Savior. And we envisioned the day when thousands who truly become acquainted with Jesus Christ, even without the aid of a missionary pastor or a church building, would begin to have an influence for Christ in their country: a spiritual "fifth column," a little leaven, that by the power of God's Spirit would reach those to whom no foreign missionary could go.

How we would like to be able to report that everything we envisioned came to pass! But our days of ministry in Lebanon were to be cut short as unrest and civil war came to that country. Most of the lands reached through the Middle East Outreach literature are still closed to missions and missionaries. We cannot give reports on what is happening today in these countries, as such reports would jeopardize faithful national workers, many of whom minister under the threat of beatings, imprisonment and even death. But the seed was sown in abundance, and it still bears fruit!

Reports have come to me from missionaries in Lebanon that during the lull between the civil war and the invasion of Israel, groups of young people were sent out into the villages to do evangelistic work. They reported back that from village to village they had found our former students. Many of them were still faithfully serving the Lord. They were eager to know what had happened to our ministry and when it would start up again, so that they could study more Bible courses. God's Word continues to reap harvest in Lebanon and the Middle East!

But in 1976 the civil war in Lebanon had brought to a standstill the channels of communication that we had utilized so effectively to distribute our literature. However, the new openness to America and Americans initiated by President Sadat in Egypt enabled us to continue some ministry through offices in that country and through another office opened in southern Europe. In spite of the efforts we had made through the years to keep as low a visibility as possible, and partly as a result of the civil war in Lebanon, various news media in the Middle East began to give front page publicity to our ministry. This was coupled with threats against my family, which now included Hazel, our two sons, and our daughter, Kim, who was born in Beirut in 1970. There were also threats against my colleagues and against my own life.

To this point, the Holy Spirit had directed me from the age of seven in what seemed to be an ever-widening circle of ministry. But now, as the attacks and publicity increased, I saw my presence and leadership hindered, and in fact, jeopardized the work that we had labored so diligently to begin. There were perplexing months, once again, of wondering and searching to know what the Holy Spirit would direct us to do next.

Even as I sought God for direction in my ministry, back in the United States another vital ministry was going through a time of transition. Our Division of Foreign Missions had reached the decision that its Spanish literature publishing center, *Editorial Vida*, which had experienced great blessing and success in the distribution of Spanish literature, should be enlarged to include publication and distribution of literature in other major languages. This decision was being made at the same time the director of *Editorial Vida* had announced his resignation and retirement. Our missions leaders, knowing of my vision for reaching a lost world through literature, asked me if I would prayerfully consider taking the reins of leadership in this growing literature ministry. With an international outreach, it would soon be known as *Life Publishers International* (LIFE). Once again, I responded to the challenge to reach a lost and dying world with the Truth of the Gospel through the medium of literature.

Chapter III

THE CHALLENGE TO TRUTH

*"For the wrath of God is revealed from heaven against all ungodliness and unrighteousness of men, who hold the **truth** in unrighteousness...who changed the **truth** of God into a lie, and worshipped and served the creature more than the Creator."*

Romans 1:18, 25

Every Communist is to be actively engaged in the distribution of atheistic literature.

Lenin

The most powerful means of propagating Communism is the small pocket pamphlet.

Leon Trotsky

5
SITTING IN DARKNESS
WITHOUT A CHOICE

It is not presumptuous to believe that God wants us to launch out in faith and fulfill the command to give the gospel to every creature. There is no presumption involved when we state by faith that we want to saturate our world with the gospel of the Lord Jesus Christ. It is not presumptuous because the Lord *commanded us to do it*!

As impossible as it might seem to us to go into all the world and preach the gospel to *every person*, it is not impossible with God. And it is not presumptuous to *believe* over all the earth, and He will be faithful when we respond to that command. He will provide all the power, anointing, financing, equipment, and everything else necessary to complete the task. God will do it. And people will respond. The gospel message is irresistible. We have seen many evidences of this truth.

Years ago, on the streets of a large city in South America, some young people were passing out tracts that were published by LIFE. A man whom we will call *Carlos*, returning home after a hard day's work, passed the young people and they thrust a tract into his hand. He glanced at it, realized that it was something religious, and ripped it into dozens of little pieces which he threw into the wind with a curse. Carlos had decided at some point that he hated God, the Church, and those who represented the Church. Very probably his attitude had developed from reading Communistic literature during the time that the Marxist movement was quite active in South America.

All the way home, Carlos cursed the Church and the young people. When he arrived home, he removed his jacket and noticed there was something clinging to it. He pulled the object off and saw that it was a small piece of the tract that he had torn up. On that little piece of tract were the words, *"And the Lord said..."* Carlos read the phrase, then pitched the paper away with another curse. But the phrase stuck in his mind.

"And the Lord said..." It echoed inside him while he ate his supper. It played on his thoughts as he tried to drift off to sleep that night, and it captured his curiosity. In fact, he really didn't sleep well at all because he kept waking and wondering what it was that the Lord had said!

All the next day as Carlos went about his work, the phrase haunted him: "And the Lord said..." Moment by moment, in spite of his denials, his curiosity mounted. Finally, as soon as his work day was over, he quickly found his way back to the same street corner where he had been given the tract. And there he found the young Christians again, faithfully giving out gospel materials, spreading the message of the gospel.

Carlos rushed up to one of the young men, and pleaded, "Please, please, tell me what it was that the Lord said." Then he described what had happened, and the young man in turn explained what the Lord said. As a result, Carlos was wonderfully saved right there on the street corner. Today, he is a pastor in South America. His story is a dynamic example of the power of the printed page!

In the Middle Ages, Europe was languishing in darkness and decadence. It was the light of God falling on the heart of a German monk, Martin Luther, inspiring him to get the Word of God into the language of the people, that literally spear-headed the Reformation. It is not by coincidence that Martin Luther's revelation and inspiration occurred simultaneous to the invention of the movable-type printing press by Gutenberg. Now, for the first time, the masses had access to the Word of God. Before that time it had been available only in hand-copied manuscripts in the obscure Septuagint, which for the most part were kept in monasteries in chains and were absolutely inaccessible to common folks. It was that access to the written word that spear-headed the Reformation. It lifted Europe out of darkness and thrust the gospel message forward.

From the point where God first wrote on the tablets with His finger, through the Old Testament and the New Testament to the Reformation, the written Word, the published Word, has been God's method. But the initiative, the drive to print, to publish, to saturate the world with the printed message has been, to a great extent, wrestled from the Church. That initiative to feed the world's people with God's Truth has been side-tracked in this century by countless forces, such as cults and communism.

One of the most intimidating world forces which attempted to bring Christian printing presses to a standstill was Communism. Down through the years as I traveled the world, I used to see Communists at work everywhere, spreading their poison in every continent on earth. Unlike many Christians, Communists weren't afraid to preach their message wherever they could get an audience. And they knew the power of literature.

A missionary in China was forced to leave in 1948 when all the missionaries were driven out of China by the Communists. He explained what really happened. He said that the Communists didn't win control of China in 1948, because they already owned it well before then! He stated that as early as 1926, in the province where he was ministering, he saw bundle after bundle of Communistic literature channeled through the postal system, and then distributed to the young people. He said that 1948 was merely a "mopping up" operation - the Communists had already won China because they had won the minds of the young people, and they had done it through literature.

In India, a nephew of Gandhi has been quoted as saying, "The missionaries came to India and taught us how to read. But the Communists came and gave us the literature to read." For all its failings, Communism's emphasis on literature shows that Communists understood the power of the printed page, especially the power it holds for someone who has just learned how to read.

From the end of World War II until the 1980's, the Communists conquered an average of 872 square miles of this earth every day. Not every year, or every month, or even every week - but *every day*! Every day they were grabbing an average of 872 square miles of territory and all the people living there! And they were doing it through literature saturation.

During the Cold War, we were concerned about the arms race and Russia's military maneuvers in the Middle East and Central America, but Communism's best weapons were always *words* - the power of the printed page!

That's how they brought one-third of the world under Communist control before the fall of the USSR. And it was expensive: it was estimated that the Communistic effort worldwide expended eight to twelve billion dollars every year just to print and distribute its propaganda.

In Peru, this investment paid off with a Marxist revolution. One of those revolutionaries was Evars Segura. He thought he was doing the right thing to destroy public property, attack police cars, even try to destabilize and overthrow the government of his homeland, Peru.

What convinced him that he was right?

Books.

In high school, one of Evars' teachers was a Marxist. This teacher gave Evars books and literature about Communism. He sent Evars off to university where there were more books, booklets and pamphlets which convinced him more than ever that Communism was the answer for his country.

It wasn't that Evars was a bad guy. It was just that he had seen his family struggle against crushing poverty in Peru.

"I became convinced the only way to change society and injustice was through taking up arms and destroying the segments of society who were oppressing the people," Evars says.

He learned all that from the books he read at school.

Evars joined a national movement of Communist terrorists in Peru. He had been prepared "as an instrument of ideological training," Evars says. "In these circumstances, my heart was being filled with hate."

The hate exploded in a burst of anti-government terrorist activities; Evars and eight of his comrades were arrested and imprisoned on charges of attempting to destabilize the government, destruction of public and private property, attacking government vehicles, and more.

Evars' family continued to love and support him. They tried every means they knew to free him; lawyers failed, even a general in the armed forces tried and failed to have him released. Then came the worst news of all.

Evars would be sentenced to the "fronton," a prison reserved for the most dangerous criminals. It is nearly impossible simply to survive alongside the cruel inmates of the fronton, but Evars learned he wouldn't even be given that slim chance.

A prison rumor indicated that Evars and his companions would be killed by prison guards, their deaths passed off as the results of an escape attempt!

The night before his formal sentencing to the fronton, Evars Segura felt a terrible fear of his own approaching death. In the books, it had sounded glorious to give his life for the struggle. But face to face with the opportunity, it did not feel glorious.

"My mother and father were Christians," says Evars. "Since I was a child, they had raised me in Sunday School, but when I was in high school I turned away because of Marxist indoctrination. In prison my mother's words about God came to me as my only alternative."

That night, in his prison cell, Evars Segura gave his heart to Jesus Christ.

The next morning when the time came for the sentence to be carried out, instead of the fronton, Evars was sentenced to seven years of probation! A miracle of God spared him from prison and probably from death!

Evars immediately went to an evangelical church and made a public profession of his faith in Christ. From that day until this, he has been a strong witness for Jesus in Peru. And now Evars is back in the schools where he first learned about Communism - but this time he's teaching about Jesus!

Evars is our director of *Book of Hope* distribution for Peru, assisting national coordinator, Rev. Umberto Lay. Evars is telling children about Jesus every day, and putting the power of God's Word into their hands.

Of course Christianity stands against everything Communism and Marxism proclaimed. So wherever Communism was in power, Christian missionaries and preachers usually could not serve; that is still the case in China, yet there is reportedly a huge Christian revival underway!

But God had been hearing the prayers of His people for the people of Russia and Eastern Europe, locked away from His Truth behind the Iron Curtain, living on enemy ground. And He responded with a mighty blow, striking down the Iron Curtain and allowing us to flood the former U.S.S.R. and Eastern Bloc countries with His Word! But at the same time that we arrived in the former Soviet Union with God's Word, the Mormons arrived with their claims. Islam arrived with its message. Cults of all kinds arrived with their distorted doctrines. Plus the practices of materialism, drug and alcohol use, immorality, crime and violence arrived from the west, too.

The dear people who had believed in Communism and now found it a total failure were desperate for something else to believe in. Now, people all over the world, looking for answers, looking for truth, will accept the first "truth" they can find. If what the cults proclaim as "truth" reaches them first, they will accept it. It became a race for the souls of the newly freed people of former Communist nations.

Cults are exerting a growing influence against the Church. Using methods similar to those once used by the Communists, but cloaking themselves in religious jargon, cults seek to lure thousands into spiritual destruction, and *literature is their main tool in attracting converts.*

In recent years there has been a 25 percent increase in Mormonism. The Jehovah's Witnesses have increased to an adherence of three million deluded souls, up 300 percent in twenty years. Other figures indicate that there may be as many as five million people who have become members of cults such as the Hare Krishnas, Scientologists, Children of God, the Divine Light Mission, Christian Science, and other Christless groups.

The Jehovah's Witnesses have been called "a zombie-like cult of magazine and tract peddlers." They have been blinding the minds of believers and others since the Watchtower Tract and Bible Society, as they were formerly named, was founded in 1879. The founder, Charles Russell, published about 20 million books before his death in 1916. His successor, Judge Joseph Rutherford, wrote more than 100 books which have been translated into 80 languages. These attacks on true Christianity sold more than 40 million copies by the time of his death in 1941. In the past five decades, the Watchtower Society has published over *two billion* volumes of books. Its more than 8,000 missionaries have covered the globe to proclaim their motto that "Watchtower Truth (Reason) comes first, the Bible (God's Word) second."

The Jehovah's Witnesses lead the cults in distribution of devil-inspired literature, with the Mormons following closely behind. And, almost all of the cults disseminate their evil propaganda with mass-produced flyers, leaflets, newspapers, magazines, and books.

Standing on street corners or in airport terminals with their free literature, or distributing it door-to-door, the innocent-looking disciples of these "ravenous wolves" are seducing countless spiritually starved souls into their folds.

The effect of a cult leader can be overwhelmingly powerful and violently destructive, as so graphically seen in the 1978 Jonestown, Guyana mass suicide and murders. During a crusade in Guyana in 1982, I talked with Dr. Leslie C. Mutu, the government bacteriologist and pathologist who led the team of investigators into Jonestown following the Jim Jones tragedy. He told me that no television documentary could capture the full impact of the horrible event. He said the air was *charged* with the presence of evil.

The Guyana tragedy stunned the world in 1978 when 912 uprooted Californians were forced to drink cyanide-laced punch by a leader suffering delusions of grandeur. But the hideousness of the act in which mothers squirted cyanide into the mouths of their tiny babies before killing themselves might serve as a symbolic warning to all of us of the dangers of deviating from God's Truth as found in His Word. Since then, we have seen the tragic deaths of the Branch Davidian cult members right on our own soil, and the horrifying mass suicide of a Swedish death cult.

Many cult leaders are motivated by a combination of monetary greed and a lust for power over others. Some are deluded by evil spirits and believe themselves to be the messiah, the savior of their generation. People from all age groups and all levels of society have been duped into joining cults and ultimately have turned over to the cult all their money, possessions, and loyalties.

Various psychological studies of cult followers have reveled that a common characteristic, a primary motivation for joining the cult, was a desire and intense need to be loved. These people have felt rejected and alienated by society, family, and friends. And often, they've been neglected or missed by the Church; they've never heard the powerful Truth of the gospel. They've never been told that Jesus loves them and died for them. Faced with the options of loneliness and rejection, or becoming a part of a cult, these people are forced to choose without being given a real choice. They could be reached with the gospel through literature.

Cults, materialism, atheism, New Age and Red China style Communism are all powerful enemies of the Church. But God is more powerfu! If His Church will be faithful and respond to the challenge of Communism and the cults with gospel literature, thousands, even millions of people - to the ends of the earth - can be reached with the saving message of Jesus Christ.

If I might control the literature of the household, I would guarantee the well-being of the Church and State.

Francis Bacon

6
THE PERVERSION OF PRINT

You and I have watched in this century, particularly in the past 25 years, the lowering of moral standards in this country at a rate that is staggering. How often do you stop and really consider the depths to which society around us has fallen? A simple way to assess the seriousness of the problem is merely to make a list of the evils prevalent in our world:

Homosexuality. Every day in the newspapers and on television and radio, we hear reports of groups clamoring for "gay" rights. There's nothing gay about homosexuality! It's a destructive sin. Just look at the recent concerns over the rapid spread of AIDS, yet homosexuality has not diminished. Same-sex marriages are promoted openly, and lesbian parents dot the covers of national magazines. Major politicians have even called for "gay" rights from the platform of one of the national conventions.

Child abuse and incest. This is one of the most tragic aspects of our decaying morality. My heart breaks every time I read another account of children being molested, abused, and even murdered - often by their own parents. And what is more appalling is that there are even reports of some psychologists and psychiatrists who suggested incest as a method to teach children about sex!

Alcoholism and drug abuse. Those who believe that drug abuse by the very young is a thing of the past are sadly mistaken. In fact, drug abuse has increased dramatically in the last four years; 1995 statistics show surges in the use of marijuana, cocaine, even heroin - among children of every age group. Glue-sniffing and drinking codeine-laced cough syrup are also common, and many household products now carry warnings on their labels against their use other than for their intended purpose.

Alcoholism has been cited by the Center for Disease Control as the No. 1 cause of evils such as wife-beating and child abuse. The Center reports that alcohol-related car crashes are the leading cause of death in the 16-24 age group. Drunken drivers cause more deaths or injuries and other destruction than do murderers, muggers, robbers, rapists and thieves combined. There have been 250,000 deaths in the United States over the past ten years because of drunken drivers. That is more than five times the number of American soldiers who died in the Viet Nam war.

Our list could go on and on: divorce, adultery, premarital sex, violence on television, abortion, neglect of the elderly and poor, suicide, dishonesty in the marketplace, inflationary government policies and so on.

But there are two problems I want to focus on, because they have opened the door for so many other evils, and their main thrust has been through the power of the printed page. They are humanism and pornography.

Humanism. Much has been written and said recently about humanism. What is humanism? When Dr. Francis A. Schaeffer died, the Christian world lost a great spokesman against humanism. In his last book prior to his death, Dr. Schaeffer very succinctly defines humanism:

> Rightly defined, secular humanism - or human ism, or secularism, or whatever you wish to use - is not a boogieman; it is a vicious enemy. Here again balance is important by means of careful definition. The word humanism is not to be confused with humanitarianism, nor with the word humanities. But humanism is the defiant denial of the God who is there, with Man defiantly set up in the place of God as the measure of all things… It stands totally against all that the original fundamentalist stood for, and totally against what the original meaning of evangelical stood for, and totally against all that the Bible stands for.[1]

And what does this mean? Earlier in his book, Schaeffer offers this insight: "Since the prevailing world view (humanism) teaches that the final reality is a silent universe which can give no value judgments, truth as final truth, therefore, does not exist."[2]

Schaeffer continues to argue that in our present day, Christians have "accommodated" the humanist rather than "confronted" him. This has happened, states Schaeffer, because instead of Christians imposing biblical standards on society, as we should do, we have allowed the Bible to be bent into conformity with the world's culture.

A Gallup study as reported in *Moody Monthly* indicated that while interest in religion in America is growing, so is *immorality*! Said the article, "There is no doubt that religion is growing," Gallup said, "but we find... little difference in ethical behavior' between those who go to church and those who don't."[3]

What does this mean? It means the Church is not being salt and light to the world! It means we are not standing up, declaring God's Truth as the absolute Truth that it is, and that we are allowing humanism to rip the foundation right out from under our society! Humanism, in all its forms, denies the authority of God's Word in every area of life.

Humanists state that Christians have no right to impose *their* values on others. They're right! But Christians aren't imposing their values - they are judging the world by *God's* values. And that's just as it should be, and just what we have been commanded by God to do.

Where humanism takes over, values take off!

What humanists proclaim as values and rights are really license. They don't want to be restricted in their freedom to sin. And, since sinners can't stand to sin alone, they want to include as many others as possible in their sin with them. They feel if they have a majority of sinners, then sin is right! But sin is never right no matter how many say it is.

Pornography. One of the most prevalent evidences of humanism is pornography. I believe the loss of moral values that is devastating America can be traced by and large to the deadly work of pornography. It is everywhere, and it is designed to appeal to the inclinations of many types of people. There is pornography aimed at the child molester, at homosexuals and lesbians, at adulterers and at teenagers. There is pornography aimed at executives and even at the housewife! There is some kind of pornography aimed at every level of our society!

With the rapid rise of the Internet, hundreds of thousands have access to a whole new pornographic industry… one that is particularly insidious in its appeal to young children. Pornographic websites and photos are now literally at anyone's fingertips, and "chat rooms" offer would-be child molesters an ideal environment for seducing youngsters and polluting their minds without their parents ever knowing what's happened.

But "high-tech" pornography hasn't replaced

the old-fashioned kind. Next time you visit the corner newsstand or your downtown bookstore, take a close look at what's stocked on the shelves. To be sure, some of the most obvious forms of printed pornography are the "girlie" magazines. But even stores that won't carry pornographic magazines carry pornographic books, and you often don't even realize it!

Look at the shelves! Look at the titles and covers of "romance" books! Look at the titles and covers of the "bestsellers." How do the publishers describe these books? *Sensuous! Sexy! Naughty! Filled with lustful passions! Forbidden love!* And on and on and on! These books are aimed at women in every age group - from young preteen girls to adult housewives and business-women. And for the men, there are detective and western stories and other kinds of fiction that are filled with the same immoral material.

The modern novel, the cheap thriller, the romance bestseller - these are the most dangerous forms of pornography. You can call me a "book-burner" if you like, but in this century we have seen in the U.S. the growth of the modern novel, which not only condones acts of immorality and unethical behavior, but makes heroes and heroines out of those characters who are the most unethical and the most immoral. In fact, those traits are actually praised as being virtuous! This detestable literature has had its subtle effects upon the mind of the nation, including many Christians who don't recognize the danger of its subtle influence.

What about the sex and violence on television? Someone wrote the book first! What about the rising rages of abortions and incest, adultery and divorce? These immoral practices have more or less become the norm in our modern society, in part because of ideas planted in novels and magazines which glamorize sexual immorality. Readers are eager to emulate the deplorable acts of immoral characters who are depicted as having desirable and sophisticated lifestyles filled with romance and intrigue. The same holds true for corporate dishonesty and greed; it is a major theme of many of the popular books of the day, and the good guy seldom wins!

It's no wonder that the hardcore pornographers are so prevalent and have such an easy time escaping the law! The lawmakers and enforcers have been so muddled in their thinking by these other forms of subtle pornography and humanism that they can't even agree on what *obscenity* is!

Surrounded as we are by so many forms of this subtle pornography, it's no wonder that our newspapers are filled with stories of massive crimes of sex and brutality. According to psychiatrists and psychologists, when a person reads something, and then begins to fantasize about it, he soon loses sight of the distinction between the fantasy and the reality; thus he may go out and commit a heinous crime, attempting to satisfy his evil desires.

How often have we heard stories about men who were convicted of committing multiple rapes and murders; yet friends and neighbors said, "But we didn't know he was like that! He was such a nice fellow!" Yet when the authorities go into their rooms, they discover all kinds of pornographic literature! This demonic propaganda of the devil the lustful fantasies all resulted in brutal and sickening reality. This is the power of the printed page.

"Legalized" pornography is a multi-billion-dollar-a-year business. Monthly circulation of the hundreds of different magazines available reaches into the tens of millions of copies. That's every month! Billions of issues every year are flooding into the world, and they are some of the most expensive magazines available, costing up to $20 or more for a single copy. There are many pornographers who are millionaires, and they are often paraded before Americans as examples of "successful and respectable" businessmen.

In America, just as elsewhere in the world, young people are looking for Truth and so are adults. If the Church refuses to confront the culture and offer a standard, then society will turn to the humanist for answers.

Why aren't more Christian magazines available

through the newsstand? Why aren't more Christian books available on the local book racks in the grocery stores and convenience stores of America? Why aren't newspapers reporting stories about Christians coming to the rescue of their neighbors and their troubled society? What have I done to promote the spread of Christian literature?

We might ask ourselves, "How often have I been seen at work reading from my Bible during a break? How much have I given over the past year toward Christian literature evangelism? How many Bibles and Christian books have I given as gifts to non-Christian friends, neighbors, and relatives? How many subscriptions to Christian magazines have I sent to others? When was the last time my family and I read from the Bible together?"

Christians and the Church are faced with a great challenge. We have lost the initiative in literature evangelism, but we can still regain what we've lost, if we act now!

---

[1] Schaeffer, *The Great Evangelical Disaster* (Crossway Books, 1984), page 205

[2] Ibid., page 101

[3] *Moody Monthly*, July/August, 1982.

Chapter IV

THE
POWER
OF
TRUTH

*"For I rejoiced greatly, when the brethren came
and testified of the **truth** that is in thee, even as
thou walkest in the **truth**."*

3 John 1:3

If the choice were ever to be between the Bible without the teacher or the teacher without the Bible, I would unhesitatingly choose the former.

Dr. G. F. Verbeck

7
THE PERSISTENCE OF LITERATURE

Some years ago there was a paper shortage in the city of Teheran, in the country of Iran. During this time, Nassi, a young Muslim, went to the market to buy cheese. When he made his purchase, the vendor, not having regular food-wrapping paper, wrapped the cheese in a printed page. This intrigued Nassi. When he arrived home, he carefully unwrapped the cheese and pressed out the now-stained page.

Nassi began reading the soiled page. He showed it to his father, who suspected rightly that it was a page from a Christian Bible. The father warned his son against reading it or any other pages like it. But the young man was thoroughly captivated by the message he had stumbled upon.

The next day, Nassi again went to the market, and back to the same food merchant. As discreetly as possible he inquired about the mysterious page, and was told than if he would buy something else, there was more such "wrapping paper" he could have and read. So the young man bought some figs, which were wrapped in a printed page.

The next day he returned and bought some dates. Then he purchased more cheese, and on and on this went for days, until Nassi had quite a collection of Bible pages which he kept hidden from his father. Naturally, the pages were not in order, and offered only bits and pieces of information. This was frustrating to Nassi. So he searched until he found an entire Bible in the Farsi language. In just a few weeks, he was drawn to the Lord and accepted Christ as his Lord and Savior. Oh, the power of the printed page! Oh, the hunger of the world!

The effectiveness of God's written Word and gospel literature is undeniable. We saw it firsthand in the Middle East, which has been considered closed to the gospel for 1300 years. Yet, within ten years we had enrolled more than 400,000 people in a massive literature program that began with a few names and records in a shoe box! And in countries like Iraq and others which are still closed to missionaries, there are scores of groups meeting regularly in secret. They have never been visited by a missionary, but they came together through the power of the printed page.

The Bible is not just so much ink on paper. God's Word is alive and the Holy Spirit is committed to accompany His Word wherever it goes. The printed page can go where missionaries cannot go. There are places where you and I cannot go - places where our nationality, our skin color and our cultural differences will not permit us to venture. But, thank God, there is not one spot on our entire planet - not even in the entire universe - that is closed to the sovereignty of the blessed Person of the Holy Spirit!

Time after time, we have seen that if only we can get the literature proclaiming God's Truth into the hands of the people, the Holy Spirit will accompany it. Christ will be made real to them and they will be converted to Him. Churches will be planted. God's Word will take root and spread!

In Laos, during the final days of the French involvement there, an interesting chain of events took place. A French missionary in the area had a real burden to reach the tribes in the remote mountain regions, but because of Communist insurgents, he could not reach them.

One day as he was driving along a street in the capital of Laos, he saw some men from a couple of the tribes he had hoped to reach. They were recognizable in their dress. He stopped and tried to converse with them in French but they didn't speak French. So, through gestures and facial expressions, he convinced them to get into his jeep and come with him.

The missionary took the tribesmen to his home, gave them some food, and then gave them a French New Testament along with some other pieces of Christian literature, even though he knew they probably couldn't read any of it. After enjoying the missionary's kindness and hospitality, the tribesmen returned to their mountain village.

One of the tribesmen, upon his return to his village, gave his Christian literature to the only person in the village who could read - the village witch doctor! The witch doctor had learned to read and speak French at a government school.

Seven years later, there was a truce between the Communist insurgents and the French. This made it possible for the missionary to visit the mountain area he had always wanted to reach with the gospel. He traveled for three days, first by train, and then by horseback, to reach the remote tribal areas. He was astonished by what he discovered.

Seven years earlier, after the witch doctor had read the Christian literature, he accepted Christ as his Savior. He didn't keep this to himself. He began to share his new life with others in the village. As their witch doctor, he was respected, and they listened to him night after night as he read from the literature. As a result, all 57 adult villagers came to know the Lord as their Savior.

Not long afterward, some of those who had been converted to Christ said, "What about the village next to ours? Those people haven't heard this message yet." So they went to the next village and told the people there about Jesus. When they were finished there, they went to another village, and then another, and another.

When the missionary arrived, he discovered eleven remote village where the gospel message had reached, and *748 new Christians* among the tribesmen. They had no fancy church buildings, no powerful preacher, no daily television or radio programs - just one French Bible and a few pieces of Christian literature. From His Word they knew that the God who had created all things sent His Son to earth. They knew the Son of God had died in man's place and had been raised from the grave. They knew the apostle John had declared, *"Whosoever believeth in Him* (Jesus) *should not perish, but have everlasting life."* Oh, the power of God's Word to bring light!

Literature goes where missionaries cannot go. When missionaries have to leave their field of service, literature stays. And its effects go on, and on, and on.

Some years ago, I was in Rockford, Illinois to speak at a local church. On the way to the church, the pastor said, "I have a wonderful surprise for you at the service tonight. Something that will really excite you!" He wouldn't tell me anything more, and I wasn't sure what to expect.

After we arrived at the church, he said, "When you get on the platform, look down to the left and you'll see something surprising." What I soon discovered was a group of about twenty young men, all obviously of Middle East origin - Syrian, Jordanian, Palestinian, and Lebanese. "Who are these people?" I asked. The pastor replied, "You wait, they'll tell you." I was curious, to say the least.

As soon as the service was concluded these young men rushed up, greeted me, and began telling me their story. It centered essentially around one of them named Fawzi and how he had become a Christian.

During some of the most terrible days of civil war in Lebanon, Fawzi spent much of his time studying in his apartment. He was confined there most of the time because of the curfews in the country. During this time, with the shops closed and no newspapers available, Fawzi was desperate for something new to read. There were no libraries open, no bookstores where he could go for material. But occasionally there would be brief cease-fire periods when people could leave their buildings and move around on the streets. During one of these times Fawzi went out, and in the street he found great piles of refuse and garbage. He started rummaging through these piles, hoping to find something he could take back to his apartment and read while the shooting was going on. In one pile he stumbled into a whole bundle of old *Way to Life* magazines (our literature ministry in Lebanon) wrapped in twine. He felt very fortunate to find such a wealth of reading material, and he hurried back to his apartment to see what kind of magazines they were.

During the next several days of fighting, Fawzi read issue after issue of *Way of Life*, and discovered that Jesus Christ was more than a prophet who lived years ago. As a result, he accepted Christ as his Savior. He continued reading the other issues of the magazine, including the articles we had written concerning the Holy Spirit. He read about this wonderful power that came through God's Holy Spirit, and he wanted it. So Fawzi prayed and received the baptism in the Holy Spirit just as God's Word promises.

Some time later, because the universities in Lebanon were closed, Fawzi's family sent him to the United States so he could continue his education, and he settled in Rockford, Illinois. Not really understanding the gift of the Holy Spirit which he had received, he decided to find a church in Rockford that believed the same things he had read about in the discarded *Way to Life* magazines. Whoever had thrown out the magazines had clipped all the addresses and response cards out of them. Because Fawzi didn't know who sponsored or published the magazines, he didn't know what church to approach.

Fawzi's plan to attack was simply to get a phone book, turn to the church section in the Yellow Pages, and, starting with the first church listed, begin attending them one by one, until he found a church that taught about this marvelous power he had experienced but didn't understand. Of course, the first church listed was an Assemblies of God Church - the First Assembly of God in Rockford! He called the church, found out when the services were scheduled, and attended that Sunday

morning. Halfway through the morning service someone stood and gave an utterance in tongues, and then
someone gave the interpretation. Fawzi told us that
when this happened his heart almost pounded through
his ribs with excitement - these were the people he was
looking for and he had found them on the first try!

In the following months, Fawzi was able to convince several of his friends who were students from the
Middle East to go to church with him. By the time I
arrived for that evening service in 1978, Fawzi had been
responsible for about twenty other young men coming
to the services, with many of them finding Jesus Christ
as their personal Savior. Some of them were filled with
the Holy Spirit and wanted to go back to their countries
in the Middle East as ministers and missionaries. Once
again - the power of the printed page! It goes where men
cannot go and stays when men are forced to leave.

In Chile, a 10-year-old girl named Maria was
responsible for taking care of her father, doing the cook-
ing and washing after her mother died. Her father was a
miner. When he was at work, Maria attended a little
Assembly of God Church every chance she got. The
church was located at the foot of a mountain in Central
Chile. In the church she found friendship and comfort.

While her life was difficult, Maria's real burden
was her father. After her mother's death, Maria's father
became morose and indifferent. Her efforts to get him to

go to church with her were ignored; when she tried to get him to read a Christian book the missionary pastor had given her, he refused, saying that he had no time for such nonsense. But one night, as she prepared food for her father's lunch pail, Maria slipped in a little book that told of Jesus' love and salvation. She prayed that night, "Oh, Jesus, please help my father to read the book so he might be saved."

At 1:10 that morning, an explosion shook the little mountain village awake as sirens began screaming into the night air. The villagers, including Maria, hurried to the mine to discover workers rushing about frantically. There had been a terrible cave-in, and Maria's father was trapped inside along with a number of other miners.

The workers dug at the fallen debris through the night and all the next day, trying to find survivors. Finally, they reached an inner chamber where Maria's father and a group of other men were located. All of them were dead - they had suffocated. But the rescuers saw a strange sight.

The men were found sitting in a circle, all eight of them. On the lap of Maria's father was a small book. It was open to the last page. Maria's father had scrawled out a message to his daughter. "My darling Maria, when you read this I will be with your mother in heaven. I read the little book by the light on my helmet, then I read it several times to the men while we waited to be rescued. Our hope has faded for this life, but not for the next. We did as the book told us, and prayed, asking Jesus into our hearts. I love you very much, Maria, and one day soon, we will all be together again in heaven."

The power of the printed page is profound. For 16 years, as president of *Life Publishers*, I was taught and prepared by God to understand and appreciate the power of His Word. The stories are endless which tell how lives have been changed by gospel literature - and not just through the work of *Life Publishers*. Perhaps even more so through the new ministry to which God has called me, of which I'll share with you in the next chapters. But first things first.

When I was leading the ministry of *Life Publishers*, we received a call from a chaplain in the prison system in Puerto Rico. He described to us the utterly deplorable conditions there and how men were often murdered in their cells as they slept. He believed if he could get some Bibles into the hands of the prisoners it would make a difference, and he asked if we could help. We said *yes*, and we sent him several thousand Bibles. In less than three months he reported to us that 750 men had given their hearts to Jesus as a result of receiving Bibles. He later sent us a list of names of former prisoners who are now going into the ministry.

Some time ago, LIFE's Mexico distributor was in Miami. He received a call from a Jewish Levite in

Mexico City who told how he had accepted Jesus Christ as Messiah after reading one of our inspirational books. Our distributor was so excited that he wanted to hang up the phone so he could report this news to everyone in our office, but the Jewish man said, "Wait a minute, wait a minute! There's more!" He went on to say that he had gone to the bookstore and bought every one of our books he could find. One of the books was on the subject of the Holy Spirit. The Jewish Levite said that as he read the book, he received the Holy Spirit baptism! Now our distributor *really* wanted to hang up the phone and start *shouting* through the offices! But again, the Jewish man said, "I'm still not through!"

He described how he started inviting other Jewish men into his home in Mexico City, to share the Good News with them. He gave them literature to show the way to eternal life. And now there were seven Jews saved and filled with the Spirit, and they were believing that God was going to pour out His Spirit on the entire Jewish community in Mexico City! Finally, our distributor was able to hang up the phone, share the news with us, and we had a praise fest!

The power of the printed Word - the effectiveness of the gospel message in print - that is something to shout about!

There are countless other instances where people have found God solely through the written message.

And it isn't strange for this to be true. Literature ministries have valuable benefits unique to the printed page.

The written Word can be studied secretly in solitude in societies that would imprison someone preaching in public. The written Word can be pondered quietly, at the reader's own pace, until the Truth takes root in his heart and mind. And God has chosen the written Word to perpetuate His self-revelation to mankind through the ages.

Another benefit of literature is that in areas where the Bible and other Christian literature are introduced, the planting of churches and great spiritual blessing follow. Many authorities on church growth attribute the amazing growth of churches in Brazil and other South American countries to the strong emphasis on prior Bible distribution as a first step in church planting.

We have seen the same in our ministry with the *Book of Hope*, a children's Scripture book which we present to the youngsters right in their schoolrooms. In 1993, we first began such distributions in the nation of Peru, which was still reeling from more than a decade of civil war. The Lord opened the doors for us to begin reaching students in the cities of Cuzco, Iquitos and Huanaco, where the pastors and believers rallied around the ministry and presented the Gospel to the children of each city. We were elated with their response, especially because Christians had been so horribly persecuted during the civil war. These days, many Christian leaders who stayed in their villages to minister during occupation by the Maoist rebels are now regarded as Maoists themselves! There is also a great spiritual oppression because of the return to ancient pagan religions among the nation's indigenous Indian population. And, the New Age movement's focus on the mystical powers of the ancient ruins at Machu Pichu is also a factor.

How wonderful to discover a thriving church in this nation, focused on evangelism! Yet when I met Pastor Eleazare Soria, I understood. Pastor of a non-denominational church in Lima, Pastor Soria's congregation focuses on intercessory prayer and combating spiritual warfare. As God reveals the names of target cities for evangelism to Pastor Soria and his staff, the church sends teams to the cities for intercessory prayer to tear down spiritual strongholds and to unite Christians in each city. In 1996, they had this active ministry in the cities of Cuzco, Iquitos and Huanaco - the same cities where we had begun *Book of Hope* distribution among the children! God had prepared the hearts of His people and the soul of each city for His Word!

We heard many miracle stories from Peru during our first efforts there, including this one from Pastor Elmer Sabaleta who grew up in the remote mountain village of Jaen. He had a deep burden to bring the *Book of Hope* to the children of Jaen, for they are cut off from the rest of the world by their geography and desperately need the Word of God. The first part of Pastor Sabaleta's journey was aboard a bus - but he was told at the bus-stop that he would have to wait for the next one. He was anxious to be on his way, but could not convince the driver to let him board.

When his bus finally came and began the long climb into the mountains, they came upon the first bus, which had been ambushed by armed bandits on the narrow, treacherous road. There was no way to "hide" the second bus, yet the robbers did not seem to notice it! They had tied up the passengers of the first bus, took their belongings, and then hurried away while the second bus waited just a little way down the road. When the passengers from the second bus came to help the robbery victims, they asked why the robbers had not attacked *their* bus. The victims replied, "They didn't seem to be able to see it!" Pastor Sabaleta says God protected his bus for the sake of His servant - and his precious cargo: two boxes filled with the *Book of Hope* for the children of Jaen.

Pastor Sabaleta loaded the books on the backs of two donkeys for the hike into the village of Jaen. The school authorities had given him permission to bring the *Book of Hope* to every schoolchild in the city. Pastor Sabaleta and his father led the donkeys from school to school where they were welcomed and asked not only to give the book to the children, but also to explain the plan of salvation! Already many students have been born again because of this outreach.

F. C. Glass, a pioneer in missionary Bible and literature distribution, made this statement, "In dozens of places where I sold the first copies of the Scriptures the people ever saw, there are strong evangelical churches today ...it was almost invariably the case where the Bible came first ... then later the preacher. I cannot recall a single incidence where the Bible came second. Speaking from personal experience, I would therefore say that if you want to open up a new area, the first thing to do is send them a Bible."[1]

[1]Watkins, Morris, *Literacy, Bible Reading,* and *Church Growth*, William Carey Library, South Pasadena, California, 1978.

If new literates cannot get good literature they will read bad literature.

Margaret Wong

Whatever is sown in these minds, the world will reap.

Frank Laubach

8
SENDING THE WORD INTO THE WORLD

Can there be any doubt about the power of the printed page to influence and hold the minds of men? God's great Kingdom plan has been carried forward through the century by the written Word. Yet we have seen that in our time this tool with inestimable power has also been used to damn and destroy men. Enslaving political ideologies, corrupting pornographic material, atheistic philosophies, and deceiving cults all seems to have grabbed the initiative away from the people of God.

It is time for the Church of Jesus Christ to intensify its efforts, to move back into the forefront of printing and publishing. The challenge of covering this planet with gospel literature is an immense one.

As we saw earlier, Jesus has commanded us to go into all the world and take His message of salvation to every person. Was He joking? After all, there are now more than 6 billion people on this globe! Surely, someone may think that Jesus had to be joking! He must have been speaking metaphorically, or something. No, Jesus meant what He said quite literally. We are to take His Truth into all the world to every person. But the good news is that His Holy Spirit prepares the way and anoints the literature everywhere we take it! Yes, there is much to do, but nothing is impossible - *with God*. In this century, world population has outstripped our comprehension. If we had begun winning converts at the rate of one per minute since the day Jesus arose, we would have won only one billion souls from then until today. Obviously, that is not fast enough to complete the Great Commission.

Suppose we could win 3,000 souls a day as the disciples did at Pentecost. How long do you suppose it would take to win more then six billion people on the earth. Over 5,480 years! If Abraham had won 3,000 converts every day and his descendants had continued to do so, it would still take us until 3000 A.D. to evangelize just the people who are now living on the earth.

Throughout the history of mankind, God's written Word has proven itself powerful in evangelism and in the establishment of God's Kingdom. This certainly should not surprise us, for God Himself has given us His promise regarding the potency of His Word. He says, *"So shall my Word be that goes forth from my mouth; it shall not return to me empty, but it shall accomplish that which I purpose, and prosper in the thing for which I send it"* (Isaiah 55:11 RSV).

Right now there are nearly 3 billion people on this planet untouched by the gospel of Jesus Christ. Yet Christ said clearly to go to *all* the world. And I say again, it is not presumptuous to believe that it can be done. It must be done! It will be done! If it were truly an impossible task, Jesus Christ would never have commanded us to do it. It is not an impossible dream to see the world saturated with gospel literature. It is possible because we have been commanded, and we are compelled to go, to work, to send the literature, and it is possible because we have been promised the support and power of God's Holy Spirit in the accomplishment of this goal.

However, obeying Jesus' command will never be accomplished by ordinary methods. It will never be accomplished just by hoping it will happen. It will only be done when the Church rolls up its sleeves and says. "With God's anointing, we are going to finish the task. We are going to saturate our world with the glorious news of Jesus' saving grace. We are going to hasten that moment when Christ shall return.

We can't be sure exactly how many people are being reached daily with the message of Jesus Christ, but let's say there are at least 50,000 (probably a very conservative estimate) who hear the Word for the first time each day. Suppose that there are five billion non-Christians on the earth. To reach all of them, we'd have to communicate to 750,000 more people every day with the Good News. Now, the Assemblies of God has been one of the fastest-growing churches both in the United States and overseas for many years. The total new converts *annually*, however, is only a few more than the people we would have to reach every day if we are to evangelize the entire world. If only 50,000 are being reached each day, then there are 700,000 every day who are not being reached! Our task is enormous.

To entertain the idea that we can win the world with one-on-one evangelism alone is short-sighted. Yes, we need missionaries, teachers, pastors, and dedicated Christians working face-to-face with those who need Jesus Christ. But it isn't enough. As we've already seen, even if we could train enough people to send them out all around the globe to every nation, there still are nations whose doors are closed to *people.* But where people cannot go, or where people are forced to leave, the printed page can go and remain. The power of the printed gospel is the most effective answer to global saturation with God's Word of redemption and love.

Think of the lives of other people all over the world; think of their needs. Imagine yourself inside the body of one of more than a billion people who fall asleep each night hungry and cold. Shut your eyes tightly and see what the blind see. Listen in a soundproof room and try to imagine what it's like to be deaf. Try to feel the agony of bodies wracked with disease and malnutrition. Hurt in your heart with those from broken homes. Imagine the world of these people, a world that offers only emptiness and despair, without Christ, without hope. All of these terrible situations are but symptoms of the world's most devastating problem - being lost without Christ.

You can feed people, and we should, but without Christ they will still be hungry. You can give medical attention, and we should, but without Christ they still need healing. You can teach people skills to help them improve, and we should, but without Christ their lives still will have no purpose. But if we give them Christ, then they discover the *source* for all their other needs!

Every day approximately 365,000 babies are born, and 150,000 people die - many without ever having had the chance to make a choice to serve the Lord because they never heard! This is a potential of over 104 souls lost to eternity every minute of every day. Or, we could say it represents an opportunity to reach 365,000 new souls every day.

Did you know that approximately 2,000 people starve to death every hour? That's more than 17.5 million people per year. Billions more are starving spiritually, choking on the lies they're fed by Communists and other anti-God forces. How many of those dying today from malnutrition, while you're reading this book, will die also of spiritual hunger, never having been told about Jesus Christ? And what will you do about all those born as you are reading this book? How many of them will grow up and die 30, 40, 50, 60, 70, 80 or more years from now, never having been reached with the gospel?

We face two choices: we must either get on with the task of reaching the lost through effective Christian literature evangelism, or we should come up with some very good excuses for why we didn't when we face our King on the day of judgment.

During my tenure at *Life Publishers*, I saw the impact of gospel literature in the lives of people. Some books, such as the Spanish translation of *The Cross and the Switchblade*, have been distributed by the hundreds of thousands, and statistics show that from five to eight people will read each book distributed.

Several years ago, a musical superstar named Barry McGuire, well known for his hit record entitled, "The Eve of Destruction," was walking along a street in California in a drunken stupor. As he stumbled along, a young "Jesus-person" passed him, and thrust a New Testament into Barry's hand. Barry looked down at the book and read the title on the cover, *Good News for Modern Man.* He said, "Hey! I'm a modern man, and I could surely use a little good news." So he took the book home with him, but never read it.

Months later, after another long period of partying and drinking, Barry noticed the book lying under his piano. For some reason he felt compelled to read it, so he did. And as he read the book, the Holy Spirit (who always accompanies God's Word wherever we send it), made Christ real to Barry McGuire. Today, he's singing songs for Jesus and is out leading thousands of young people to Christ. This is the power and potential of the printed page.

As I have shown in the preceding chapters, the power of the printed page to spread the gospel and touch men's hearts is absolutely undeniable. Christian literature anointed by the Holy Spirit is always effective, and the only way, I believe, that we will be able to fulfill Christ's injunction to reach all the world.

It is equally undeniable that there is a vast need for God's Truth in the world. Billions are without Christ. Billions have never heard or read about Jesus. These are *people*. People as countless as the stars. Carl Sagan, a humanistic astronomer and scientist, often expressed his awe over the "billions and billions" of stars in space. Yet in spite of his awe, Sagan continued to deny God's existence, as far as we know, until his death. The vastness of God's creation didn't move him to believe.

We are in many ways just like this godless scientist. We are awed by the numbers - the billion and billions of lost souls - but we, too often, are not moved to act. And what is our excuse?

Some say the problem is too big - there are too many people and we'll never be able to reach them all. But to say those things is to deny the reality of what we have seen accomplished through gospel literature.

We *can* reach everyone everywhere on this planet with God's redeeming message. We can and we must. But we must do it together.

And now God has given us a perfect tool for world evangelization. It's a simple children's book called the *Book of Hope*.

Chapter V

PUBLISHING THE TRUTH

*"When he, the Spirit of **truth**, is come, he will guide you into all **truth**"*

John 16:13

Evangelism, the foremost mission of the Church, finds no more effective key than the printed word - primarily the Bible and secondarily all books which draw the reader by whatever path to think about God.

Ruth Ure

9
TRUTH BY THE TON

It was a sad parting… but I knew God was calling me onward and upward. God had blessed and prospered the work of *Life Publishers* as I led the ministry for 16 years. But a few years ago, I could see that my mission there was complete; we had published millions of Bibles, books, study materials and Scripture portions in the French, Spanish and Portuguese languages. We had Bibles for children and youth, as well as a variety of study Bibles for pastors such as *The Thompson Chain Reference Bible* and the *Full Life Study Bible*. And what's more, other Bible publishers had begun to serve the Spanish, French and Portuguese-speaking worlds. The need for which I had originally been called to *Life Publishers* was being met, and I began to pray about being released from this responsibility.

I consulted with the Division of Foreign Missions, and we agreed that it was time to put *Editorial Vida* (Spanish, French and Portuguese editions from Life Publishers) into the hands of a commercial publisher. The work was sold to Zondervan, with the proceeds earmarked to begin fulfilling other publishing needs within the denomination. A new *Life Publishers* would continue the publishing of curriculum material, the *Full Life Study Bible* and needed study books. But as for me, God had called me to something totally new and incredibly exciting!

Beginning in 1987, God had put a new call on my life and heart.

This powerful new ministry came to be known as *Book of Hope International.*

I believe it can be the key to world evangelization as Christ commanded.

Let me explain.

God burdened me for the lost children of the world, but I did not know how I could possibly help them. I could clearly see that all the wars, the famines, the proliferation of sexual promiscuity, the drugs and alcohol were aimed at destroying the next generation. But what could I do?

When my father helped me launch my ministry at seven years of age, there was a tendency for people to think I should preach to other children. But God had told me my message was for everyone, not just children. So I resisted that idea and for most of my life as a minister and missionary, I did not focus on children.

That's why it was so strange to me that over a period of six weeks in 1987, God gave me a vision of the children and youth of the world. He showed me that the children and youth of the world were Satan's number one target - that the great spiritual battlefield for the world right now is taking place for the minds and hearts and souls of the youth.

It is not difficult to understand that when you realize statistics show 80% of all believers accept Christ before the age of 18, most before the age of 14. By the time young people reach their late teens, their minds have been filled with all kinds of philosophies, theologies or ideologies. By then, Satan has succeeded in ensnaring most with the chains of immoral habits, and it becomes more and more difficult to make a decision for change.

Why would Satan target the children and the young people? That also is easy to understand when you realize that although Satan is not omniscient - only God knows the future - the devil does have as much under-standing about the future as we humans have. He truly knows that importance of Jesus words in Matthew 24:14, *"And this gospel of the Kingdom shall be preached in all the world for a witness unto all nations; and then shall the end come."* What does the end mean for Satan? That also is clear in God's Word and the devil surely understands that at the return of Christ, his free-dom to rule as the prince of the power of the air will be taken from him. That it means he will be bound, cast into a bottomless pit never again to be free, to oppress, to hurt and to destroy.

So Satan actually fights for his own survival. If he can destroy the next generation, if he can keep the children from hearing the good news about Jesus, then he will elongate his reign of terror. Of course, Satan also knows how open and responsive the children are to the love of Jesus Christ. As I understood that, I began to survey the disasters, the calamities around the world, and more and more I saw the evil being directed toward the children.

I still remember a few years back when I saw the article in *Time Magazine* about the exploitation of children in worldwide sex trade. It tore at the burden in my heart for little ones around the world. The stories in the article told about:

> * Little 8-year-old Marik, one of the thou-
> sands of Moscow's "throw-away" kids,
> who was sold for a case of vodka to a
> pimp named Sasha. He dresses Marik up
> like a girl and sells him to pedophiles on
> the streets of the Russian capital. Sasha
> has two other little boys working for him,
> and he says they're happy to do it because
> he feeds them and provides a place for
> them to live.
> * Beautiful Manju was a 12-year-old
> Nepalese girl whose father sold her to
> white slavers when her mother died. Eight
> years later, she was working in a brothel in
> Bombay and could foresee no other way of
> life for herself.
> * Marie, in India, is a barefoot 12-year-
> old child in a wedding dress, hoping some-

one will "marry her and save her from her mother's fate - a brothel," the article said.

* The statistics of child sexual abuse in other nations - such as Sri Lanka and Thailand where child prostitution is a multi-million dollar industry - are terrible; it's estimated that half the child prostitutes are infected with the AIDS virus.

* One of the tragic by-products of Communism's fall in Eastern Europe is this: thousands of young women turn to prostitution in hope of making enough money to survive. One law enforcement official said, "The naivete is unbelievable. The vision of earning hard currency blurs these girls' senses."

* Some U.S. and European travel agencies and publications are devoted exclusively to helping pedophiles find exotic vacation spots where they can legally abuse children. Around the world, babies are the victims of adult lust; youngsters are bought and sold - as one trader put it, "like a kilo of bread."

My heart breaks to think of these innocent children, kidnapped and enslaved. Much of this horrifying trade is the result of poverty. But I know first hand that in places like the former Soviet Union - where there has been so little Judeo-Christian teaching for an entire generation - young girls actually look at prostitution as a glamorous career.

In fact, Russian high school girls ranked prostitution #8 on a list of preferred careers. They look at it like another career option, like nursing, teaching, or flying airplanes; only they look at it as a more lucrative option than those others.

This is a tragedy of epic proportions.

When I think about it - not just a minister of the Gospel, but as a father - I'm angered... and saddened... I cry.

If you are a parent or grandparent, I know this must break your heart as well. I cannot help but think of my own beautiful daughter, and my precious granddaughters. I would die myself rather than allow anything so horrible to happen to them.

So I cannot help but imagine the heartbreak of the parents and grandparents of these precious children around the world who are being abused in this deplorable practice.

When I read about the blonde, blue-eyed Russians who have become so common as call-girls in areas of Turkey and the Black Sea that they are referred to collectively as "the Natashas," I think about all the blonde, blue-eyed little girls in the schools of Russia.

Those "Natashas" are their older sisters, their play-mates. And how many of them will follow in their sisters' footsteps if we don't intervene?

God broke my heart over a period of weeks. The feeling was so strong that Hazel and I could be sitting in a restaurant and if a mother and children walked by, I would begin to weep. I even wept when children came on television. What could it mean?

Dale Berkey, my good friend and prayer partner, joined me in prayer and fasting for a clear revelation of God's purpose. And the message that God revealed was this: I want My Word taken to the children and youth of the world, but you will have to begin with world leaders.

I didn't know any world leaders, but that information was easy to obtain. We made a gift of our beautiful Spanish-language Study Bible to each of the top 50 leaders in many Spanish-speaking nations. We embossed their names in gold on the cover and delivered them to presidents, vice-presidents, premieres, bank presidents, and telecommunications leaders.

Amazingly, I began to get thank-you calls from these leaders! The president of Chile even invited me to visit him and ended up placing an order for a Study Bible for every member of his cabinet and staff. I was invited to the presidential palace of Venezuela, and then one day I received a cable from a minister of religion in the country of El Salvador.

He wrote to thank me for the Bible, but he went on to say, "As you probably know, our nation suffered years of civil war. We have the highest murder rate in the world, and it is the innocent ones - the children - who are suffering the most. How I wish every one of them could have themselves a copy of God's Word."

And then the big question: "Mr. Hoskins, if it is possible, could you supply Bibles for all the children in our public school system?"

It was a wonderful request! But how ironic: in the United States, founded by our Christian forefathers, our Supreme Court has said we can't even read the Bible to the children in the public schools.

Yet here is a minister of state asking me to bring God's Word into the classroom for every single child in the nation!

I was so thrilled, I sent a telegram immediately: "YES! We will provide the Word of God for every schoolchild in El Salvador."

I didn't even know how many schoolchildren there were in El Salvador.

It turned out there were 968,000 children of reading age in their school system!

Then I really started fasting and praying: "Oh Lord, where will I get a million Bibles? What am I going to send these children?"

We wanted to give them something they could

read and understand right from the start, so I didn't think an entire Bible would do - even theologians struggle with some parts of it. I didn't think children would understand it at all.

What they could understand and what they needed to know first was: God loves you and has a plan for your life. And that is illustrated throughout the life of Christ.

So we followed God's leading to harmonize the gospels of Matthew, Mark, Luke and John so that nothing was repeated, and nothing was left out. The life story of Jesus was told in chronological order, an easy-to-understand story made up entirely of Scriptures. His birth, life, teaching, miracles, crucifixion, resurrection and ascension are all included, along with the first two chapters of the Book of Acts to introduce the power of the Holy Spirit who is always with us and empowers us.

Then, to be absolutely sure that the salvation message was clearly presented, we added 100 programmed questions that would take the student back to key verses again and again. These verses reinforce who Jesus is, who God is, what sin is, who the devil is, what it means to believe on Christ and call on the name of the Lord. Finally, we added a sinner's prayer and a plan of salvation. We wrapped it all up together and in Spanish we called it *"El Libro de Vida."*

We had the tool!

But we didn't have the money to print and ship nearly a million of these little books. God opened hearts to this mission. Friends responded. Churches responded. People gave again and again, sacrificially, to provide those funds. And by December 1987, we were able to send 1 million copies of *El Libro de Vida* to El Salvador. The shipment filled nine freight cars and weighed 128 tons.

Thankfully, the Christians of El Salvador organized by John Bueno, one of this century's great missionaries, had volunteered to distribute the books. They were so thrilled to have this gift of God's Word for their children, that they used their own cars, pickups, jeeps, motorcycles, bicycles, canoes, and even horses and donkeys to go into every town and to reach every school. They went up into mountains and down into valleys. They carried the books on foot and balanced boxes of books on top of their heads.

They carried a letter from the government to show each school that they had authorization to give God's Word to the children. But the school directors wouldn't hear of their dropping off the books and moving on. "No!" they said, "You came all this way to bring the books; let's get the children together and you can explain it to them."

Without our planning it as a strategy, God opened the door for our brothers and sisters in El

Salvador to stand up in every classroom to preach the Gospel, to share their testimony, and leave God's Word with every child in that nation.

And this book was probably the only book that many of the children in rural areas had in their homes. They read it to their parents, their grandmas and grandpas, and their little brothers and sisters. An entire nation heard the good news about Jesus Christ.

The Holy Spirit accompanied the living Word. People began to give their lives to Christ. Just a few months later *Charisma* magazine reported that evangelical leaders meeting in San Salvador declared that if the ratio of revival continued, by the year 2000 it may be that 75-80% of the entire population will be born-again believers.

Well, praise God, we had reached all the children of El Salvador and God's Word was doing its missionary work. Whew! We met the challenge. Except now that we had this powerful children's book in the Spanish language, couldn't we produce a few hundred thousand more and give it to the children of Ecuador, and Costa Rica, and Nicaragua? And couldn't we translate this book into French and Portuguese? Why couldn't we do what God had commanded? Why couldn't we reach the world through those who are the most open, the most receptive… the children and young people?

The second language was French. The little

nation of Haiti asked us to bring it to their children during some of the most despairing moments of civil war there. Then the French-speaking nations of Burkina Faso and the Ivory Coast of Africa asked for the book. Next I was invited to meet with the president of Brazil to discuss reaching Brazilian children with the Portuguese-language *Book of Hope*.

Throughout all of this, friends and churches continued to support the mission with their faithfulness and prayers. The efforts were very cost-effective, for we could print each *Book of Hope* at a very reasonable price.

We did some research to discover that, with 20 languages, we could reach 90% of the readers of the world. With ten languages we could reach over 60% of the readers of the world. We prioritized a list of ten languages and we said, "As God opens the door through the leaders of these language areas, we'll put the book in those languages and do the distribution."

Then one day a friend in my office looked over the list of 10 languages and said, "Hey, you've left out one of the world's most important languages. What about Russian?"

Remember, this was early 1988: the Berlin Wall, the Iron Curtain, the Cold War. For 70 years anybody in the Soviet Union that was found to own a Bible went to prison.

I said, "Brother, if I add Russian to this list, who would believe it? We would lose all credibility. Nobody would believe anything I said after that."

Isn't God still saying to His disciples, to all of us, "Oh ye of little faith?"

So I didn't put Russian on the list. But a few months later on a Friday night, I was in prayer with some friends and God spoke through a prophetic word. That word for the *Book of Hope* was: "Russian." On Monday I was flying back to Florida to go to my office and I was thinking about this prayer meeting, wondering who that fellow was who gave the prophetic word.

I finally decided, "I don't really know that guy very well. I don't know where he came from. I don't know if that was really a word from the Lord. I better wait on this."

"Oh ye of little faith."

When I got to my office, my secretary told me that some Scandinavian brothers were trying to reach me to talk about the *Book of Hope* in Russian. Did you ever have those little hairs on the back of your neck sort of stand up?

These men were the dear brothers who had secured the first-ever, official license to take 50,000 Bibles into Russia. They said, "We've heard about this *Book of Hope*. We want this first distribution to be thoroughly evangelistic so we want to talk about using it."

I showed them the *Book of Hope* and they wanted to use it, but I had to tell them: "God's direction to me has been very specific. This book is for the children and youth of the world. If you get the opportunity to go into the schools, then I would love for you to take the *Book of Hope* for children."

I didn't think I would ever see them again.

A few months later, they were back in my office with an invitation from the Minister of Religion for the Soviet Union to come and talk about distributing the *Book of Hope*.

And that's how, on a bitter cold day in 1990, with my son Rob and some of our colleagues, two vanloads of us pulled up in front of Public School No. 715 in the heart of Moscow. We had entered the then Soviet Union the previous day as official guests of the Soviet government. We had in our possession a document from that government authorizing us to go into public schools and to give the children in those schools and others 50,000 copies of the Word of God in the form of "Kniga Zhezn," the Russian-language *Book of Hope*.

This was the first school, the first attempted distribution. We had no way of knowing what kind of reception we would have, what kind of response we would get. And now we were going to do something that we couldn't even do in your city or town, or anywhere else in the United States of America. We were going into a public school to openly give the children the Word of God.

When the big, imposing doors opened and we entered a large lobby, the first thing I saw was a twelve foot tall statue of Lenin standing there staring down at us with an awful frown on his face, obviously very unhappy that we were there.

And in just a moment, a little lady came running into the lobby. She introduced herself as the director of the school. She said, "I know a little about your mission, but please come into my office so I can better understand what you want to do." She had me seated across the desk from her.

She said, "I am by profession a history teacher and I've been teaching history in the Soviet Union now for more than 40 years; during that time, our government from time to time changes what we teach about history. Now, for the first time, we are permitted to teach the history of religion. But I am a Communist, an atheist, and I don't know very much about the history of religion. Personally, I am happy to receive this book because I'm sure it will help me better understand the history of religion."

I said, "Well ma'am, we want you to have this book, but there is a misunderstanding. This is not a book about history. This is not a book about religion. Rather this is the Word of the eternal living God. And in this

Word He tells us how we may experience His presence in our lives through his Son Jesus Christ." I then waited to see what kind of response this would get from the 60-year-old atheist history teacher.

An incredible thing happened! For a moment she looked startled, and then I saw a huge tear fill the corner of her eye. With a trembling voice she said, "You can't understand how nearly impossible it is for us to believe that." She went on to describe the plight of the Soviet Union and she said. "We do not want our children to grow up as we have grown up - please help our children have faith."

She personally escorted us from classroom to classroom where our team members shared the gospel, gave our testimonies, and left a copy of God's Word in the hands of every child in Public School No. 715.

It was an event, a miracle that I think is best described by the Word of God to the prophet Habakkuk, *"Wonder, be amazed, astonished, astounded because I will do things in your day you won't even believe when you hear about it."*

That's the miracle God provided when He gave us the *Book of Hope*!

While we were doing distribution in Moscow, we were called to another meeting with Mr. Igor Vischepan, the Minister of Religion. He told us that the permit for 50,000 Bibles was no longer valid. We were astonished. I was thinking to myself, "Isn't that just like the Communists? They break every promise they make."

But in the next breath, Igor said, "Instead of a permit for 50,000, we are giving you a request. I am requesting that you bring 140 million copies of the *Book of Hope*. We want every child in every school to have it. We want every prisoner in every prison, and every patient in every hospital, and every orphan in every institution to have it."

He went on to describe how the old Communist system was finished, and no one could really predict the future, but that they knew there would be a need for some kind of moral foundation. He said, "We must have something to help build character in our children. As a rule, moral values were previously passed down by parents, but in the Soviet era, parents didn't do it. Values and morality were imposed by the state, primarily to keep control." He went on to say it was vital that parents take up the work of teaching values, but that lots of them didn't know how to do it. They'd had no practice. So he said, "Please, can you help us by providing this book for our nation."

We were so excited as we continued distribution in the Moscow area, that we said, "We have to pick up the tempo. Let's blitz one major city after another!" We planned our blitz of the city of Leningrad's 1,586 schools, but we were told it was impossible.

Why? Because there weren't enough Christians in Leningrad to do the distribution. In other nations where we had taken the *Book of Hope*, local Christians had banded together to distribute it to the children. But here, the pastors told us, even if all the Christians got together, there wouldn't be enough to visit 1.6 million children in the schools of Leningrad in six weeks.

But then one pastor got an idea: "You have millions of Christians in America. Why don't you go back and get some Americans to come?"

The idea of *Affect Destiny* team missions was born.

I was dubious that it could work, but my son Rob and I came home and phoned a few pastors. It sounded preposterous to me even as I said it: "Do you have anybody in your church that would volunteer to go to the Soviet Union at their own expense? There aren't enough Christians in Leningrad to take our *Book of Hope* to all the schools."

Within a few weeks, we had 250 volunteers!

One of the most touching and moving sights of the past 12 years to me is still the day we launched the "Leningrad Invasion," as we called it. We had publicized a marathon race between a Russian super-marathon runner and a Finnish marathon runner. The television news and thousands of spectators had turned out for the arrival of the marathon runners and as they approached the city, the Finn held high a copy of the *Book of Hope*. We had 100 children who had already received the book run to greet him, all waving their books. By now everyone was asking, "What is this book?"

The athletes ran all the way to the steps of Smolney Cathedral, a historic site in Leningrad from which Lenin launched the Communist Revolution. Here we had a public address system set up, and we began a Bible-reading marathon.

From these steps, Lenin had called religion the opiate of the masses. He had pledged to obliterate the Bible from the Soviet Union and eventually the whole world.

Instead, from Smolney Cathedral and several other sites throughout the city, we read the entire Bible aloud, from cover to cover. For 72 hours non-stop, rotating readers every 30 minutes, we read through the whole Bible! Television was reporting it, radio was carrying it, and newspapers were featuring it.

Our first reader was the chief architect of Soviet military strategy, admiral of the entire fleet of Soviet nuclear submarines. And here this old Communist admiral stood up, and his big booming voice rang out in Russian, "In the beginning God created the heavens and the earth…" I think that in Red Square, Lenin rolled over in his tomb!

The response to all this publicity was astonishing. Every day parents crowded into the schools with their children to meet the Americans and hear about the *Book of Hope.* Children became missionaries to their families.

My son Rob realized at once that it wasn't enough just to give the book to the children - we needed an entire citywide forum to reach parents and grandparents because they were so hungry for the truth!

So God opened up the door for us to conduct crusades in halls and auditoriums. For example, when we got to Krasnojarsk, Siberia, parents and families came by the thousands. During six weeks of distributing the book in schools of Krasnojarsk and the nightly crusade in the hockey arena, we had over 68,000 signed decision cards from people who had publicly confessed Jesus Christ as their Savior!

This strategy worked across Russia, and it has changed entire cities. Krasnojarsk is a city with many churches now. This has been repeated in city after city across the old Soviet Union.

In fact, there are so many young people being born-again and being called into the ministry that they had to start a Bible school in Krasnojarsk to train the young men and women for full-time ministry. This year they will have over 100 students studying for the ministry. Before 1991, there was only a tiny nucleus of believers in that city.

If you've ever been on an *Affect Destiny* team, then you know that the hunger in the hearts of people is so incredible as to be indescribable.

When we first started going into the schools of Russia, in one classroom, one of our volunteers presented the gospel and gave the *Book of Hope* to the children. He said, "When you get home tonight and finish reading the book, there's a prayer in the back of the book which you can pray to ask Jesus to come into your heart."

A little boy raised his hand and asked, "Why do I have to wait until tonight? Can we pray right now?"

This was all new to us. We weren't sure how far we could go, because at this time there was still a Soviet Union and a Communist government. Our volunteer knew there were still exiles in Siberia, imprisoned for owning a Bible. He was thinking that the teacher was probably a Communist... but he turned to the schoolteacher and said, "Would that be all right? Can we pray?"

And the teacher said, "Oh, yes, please do. I want Jesus to come into my heart also."

In another school, the administrator stopped me on the way out after a distribution and said, "I know you're very busy, but can you spare 10 minutes to meet with the teachers and administrators?"

About 100 people had gathered, and again, this was before the fall of the Soviet Union. I was fairly sure that my audience were all Communists, so I wanted them to begin thinking first of all about the existence of God. I began to tell them some of the theological proofs of God's existence.

But the school director stopped me in just a couple minutes and said, "You're right to assume we are atheists here, because that is what we have been taught. But now we have our doubts about atheism, and we are willing to agree that God may exist. So please, we have only 10 minutes of your time. Tell us: if there is a God, how do we reach Him?"

Oh, this was the sweetest, easiest evangelism I had ever done. I was able to tell those people: "There is one name given under heaven whereby men must be saved, the name of Jesus. If you want to reach God, stand to your feet and let me pray with you." And all those teachers and administrators stood and I led them to Jesus.

There's a hunger so intense.

I'm thinking of Natasha, a 12-year-old Russian girl. All her life, her parents had taught her that there is no God. But her old grandmother, who lived in the same one-room flat her family shared, told her differently.

All her life, Natasha's grandma would tell her, "Natasha, there is a God." And every evening, Natasha heard her grandmother pray to God that He would send someone to her town with His book for Natasha.

One day, our *Affect Destiny* team came to her

school with the *Book of Hope*. One of the volunteers was Sergei, a Russian immigrant to California, who spoke fluent Russian. He presented the Gospel and told the children that this book was God's love letter to them.

Natasha could hardly wait until after the presentation so she could speak with Sergei. "Mr. Sergei," she said, tugging at his sleeve. "My grandmother has been praying for someone to come and bring me God's Word; but she prayed for many years, and no one ever came. I started to believe what my parents and my teachers told me - that there is no God. I thought my grandma was just too old and didn't understand."

But then Natasha held up her *Book of Hope* and hugged it against her chest. "I am going to run home as fast as I can to my grandma and tell her the people came - they were right here in my school - and they gave me God's book. I'll tell her, 'I have the book, Grandma, and now I know God does exist!'"

These stories are just small examples of the miracles we hear of through the *Book of Hope* ministry every day. So far, we've given the book to over 144 million children and their families in South America, Russia, Eastern Europe, the Caribbean, India, Africa, and the Philippines.

But there are millions more to be reached, million more like Natasha's grandma, just praying that someone will bring them the Truth.

Please remember we are debtors to all Bible-less people. Our lives have meaning as we make installments on the payment of the debt.

Jack McAllister

10
MEETING THE NEED AND THE CHALLENGE

God won't preach in Russia.

Can you believe that?

He expects you and me to do it.

Let me show you.

Through the *Book of Hope*, we have now covered over 300 of the major cities of the former U.S.S.R. - over 40 million children in the former Soviet Union alone, as of this writing, have received the truth found in God's Word and shared it with their families. (We've reached 144 million children worldwide). Scores of churches have been raised up from these new converts, and some of those churches are now sending out missionaries and evangelists to other countries.

For example, Pastor Edward Grabovenko of the city of Perm used the *Book of Hope* to expand his church to more than 3,000 members. He also used the book to evangelize the Perm region of the Ural Mountains and plant 100 other churches. And, he has sent missionaries from his church to China, where they use the *Book of Hope* to reach others. Many believers in his church send offerings to support the *Book of Hope* ministry to other regions of the world! If you know how incredibly difficult the economic situation is in Russia right now, then you understand what a huge sacrifice these believers are making; but they believe in the *Book of Hope*! It brought them a knowledge of Christ love.

How has all this happened? For those of us who grew up under the shadow and the terror of the Cold War, it seems that such a thing could just never be. This great, mammoth system gobbled up nearly two-thirds of the earth. Look at the record. No political analyst foresaw or foretold the collapse of Communism. Of course, after it happened, everyone was an expert.

Military authorities said it was the military situation. Economists said it was the economic situation. Politicians said it was Gorbachev. Historians said it was glasnost. I have news for them all. It wasn't the military. It wasn't economics. It wasn't politics. It wasn't glasnost. It wasn't Gorbachev. It was the almighty God.

God heard the prayers of His people. God saw the suffering of the saints in the Siberian gulags. God's heart was broken for the children who were being denied access to the Truth, and God stepped in. God intervened.

When God gets ready to intervene, it's always dramatic. Our God is an intervening God. He steps into history, and He changes its course. He directs the destinies of nations, and it's always dramatic.

When God was ready to lead the children of Israel out of Egypt, remember the plagues? Pretty dramatic, wouldn't you say? The rolling back of the waters of the Red Sea was a divine intervention.

I heard of one agnostic student of history and geography who said, "At that time, there was a place in the Red Sea which was only six inches of water, and that's where the children of Israel escaped."

I said, "It's an even greater miracle than I thought! God drowned the entire Egyptian army in six inches of water! Blessed be His name!"

No, friend, when God gets ready to open a door, He doesn't push it open a pinch. He knocks the whole wall down. He tears the curtain aside. He prepares the way, and He incites this hunger which is so intense as to be indescribable. But then, wonder of wonders, after God opens the door, after God prepares the way... remember:

God will not go preach in Russia. He will not send angels. The Bible says angels cannot tell the redemption story. Wonder of wonders! After God prepared a lamb slain from the foundation of the world, after God came Himself, submitting to the humiliation of the cross, after He arose from the dead because He is God, He declared, *"All authority under heaven and in earth is in my hands"* (Matthew 28:18 KJV). And, He proclaimed, *"Whosoever now will call upon the name of the Lord will be saved!* The price is paid! Your redemption is assured!" Then He turned to created beings like you and me, His disciples, and said, *"Now you go into all the world, and you preach the Gospel to every creature."*

The fact is, my brother, my sister, if we don't go, the lost of this world will never hear.

I prefer, rather than calling it the Great Commission, to call it the *Great Entrustment*. God has put the message of everlasting life in our hands. The going is now up to me and you.

Lest there be any misunderstanding about this great entrustment, God spoke and said to the man of God, *"When I say to a wicked man, 'You will surely die,' and you do not warn him or speak out to dissuade him from his evil ways in order to save his life, that wicked man will die for his sin, and I will hold you accountable for his blood"* (Ezekiel 3:18 NIV).

Today, as never before, the Church has the opportunity to go with the Gospel. You have the opportunity to go with the Gospel. The printed Word of God makes it possible!

Down through history, God has used the written Word to give His message to the world. Some day the task of world evangelism will be completed, and the end time events recorded in the book of Revelation will be played out. I am awed to realize the importance of books in all of these end-time events.

"And he had in his hand a little book open" (Rev. 10:2 KJV). When the mighty angel appeared in

the vision of John, the main instrument of his power was a little book. He was clothed with a cloud. He wore a rainbow on his head. His face was shining like the sun because he was a bearer of light. He stood ready for the widest usefulness, his right foot upon the land and his left foot upon the sea. In his hand, as the main instrument of his power, he held *"a little book open."* Think of it! When the angel comes to *"swear by him that liveth for ever and ever, who created heaven, and the things that therein are, and the sea, and the things which are therein, that there should be time no longer"* (Rev.10:6 KJV), he will not come with a sword of military conquest. He will not come with the methods of world commerce. He will not come with some great ecclesiastical system. But in his hand he will hold a little book!

Again, in John's vision, the seer records that he *"saw the dead, small and great, stand before God; and the books were opened: and another book was opened, which is the book of hope; and the dead were judged out of those things which were written in the books, according to their works"* (Rev. 20:12 KJV). John goes on to declare that the sea, death, and hell deliver up the dead which are in them. Finally death and hell are cast into the lake of fire.

But the words that ring in my heart as we face the challenge of the unfinished task are found in the final verse of chapter 20: *"And whosoever was not found written in the book of hope was cast into the lake of fire"* (v. 15).

I am 100 percent convinced that through mass distribution of the book God has placed in our hands, we can snatch millions from the burning who will rise up at that judgment day to call us blessed.

The means to reach the next generation around the world is in our hands today. The *Book of Hope* is a cost-effective tool for telling children and families everywhere about Jesus. It takes just 33¢ right now to place the book into the hands of a needy child.

The year 2002 marks our 14th Anniversary of *Book of Hope* ministry, and how God has blessed us! For the past 14 years, on an average, we have placed a *Book of Hope* into the hands of a child every 3 seconds of the day! Already we have reached over 144 million youngsters.

In the next 10 years, I want to see us reach 800 million.

One way that you can be part of this great mission is through your prayers, and I plead with you to pray every day for the children. We are experiencing increasing spiritual warfare. It is only through your prayers and God's faithfulness that we continue to move forward, proclaiming the good news.

Colossians 4:2-3 (NIV) makes my plea, *"Devote yourselves to prayer, being watchful and thankful. And pray for us, too, that God may open a door for our message, so that we may proclaim the mystery of Christ."* The prayers of friends like you open the doors for the Gospel, pave the way for the *Affect Destiny* teams, saturate our crusades and distributions with God's Spirit, and insure the safety of our staff and volunteers. You bring down the strongholds of Satan when you lift us up in your prayers!

In addition to your prayers, I invite you to give. Every dollar you give reaches three children with the *Book of Hope*. Where else can your dollars go so far toward world evangelism? And when we sow the seed of Gods Word into such fertile ground, we reap a great harvest of souls. Most Christians (80% or more) say they received Christ as Savior before the age of 18. Youngsters are the most tenderhearted segment of the population, open to the truth of the gospel. Your investment in telling children about Jesus is wise and will produce eternal benefits.

One way that your prayers and giving can be most effective is through the *HOPE GIVER* outreach. This dynamic program allows you to give God's Word to three school children every single day of the year.

When you make a *HOPE GIVER* commitment, you will be reaching young people like Maxim from Chernigov, Ukraine. Like some sullen teenagers, Maxim was quarrelsome and rebellious. His mother feared he would follow in the footsteps of his dad and become an alcoholic. In this despairing nation, what could change that path? The gospel of Jesus could!

Maxim read the *Book of Hope* and now he is a believer - as well as being the church pianist. He has led his sister to the Lord and is praying for his parents' salvation. Their church was started through *Book of Hope* outreach in their city of Chernigov.

You will give the *Book of Hope* to a boy like Artuom from Magnitogorsk, Russia. His mom is a follower of Hare Krishna and his father is an atheist. What hope does he have for eternity? The hope of Jesus, delivered in the *Book of Hope*! He received the *Book of Hope* at school and today he is a committed believer, sings in the youth choir, helps to lead his church youth group and witnesses to his friends!

(Oh, yes - the church Artuom attends was also launched through the *Book of Hope* in Artuom's home city of Magnitogorsk.)

You can also give the *Book of Hope* to a young lady like Irina, who lives with her 6 brothers and sisters in a gypsy village on the outskirts of Minsk, Belarus. With the severe economic struggles in the former Soviet Union, what hope is there for Irina's future? There's the eternal hope of Jesus. She received the *Book of Hope* in school, and now she is a vibrant Christian - telling her friends about Jesus and helping translate English teaching materials into Russian for her church.

When you become a HOPE GIVER, you put the *Book of Hope* into the hands of children like these all over the former Soviet Union, Latin America, Eastern Europe, Africa, Asia and around the world! Your commitment of just $1 a day reaches three youngsters like these, every single day!

I realize giving $1 a day works out to $30 a month, $365 a year, and that is a sacrificial commitment for many people. But I boldly ask for it because of the children I've met who are still waiting to receive the hope of the gospel.

I think of Nina, a Bosnian girl forced into a refugee camp with her sister and grandma. Their parents stayed behind to try to save their home, but their dad was executed by the advancing enemy.

I want to give hope to children like Nina, and I trust that you want to help, too. I believe someday we'll meet Nina in heaven and she will say, "Thank you for caring enough to give, so I could meet Jesus!"

That's not just wishful thinking. I have met so many young people in Bosnia whose lives of hatred and bitterness have been completely, miraculously transformed by the power of God's Word.

I think of Sondra, a 22-year-old Muslim woman whose father, like Nina's, was killed in the Bosnian conflict. Sondra grew up angry and afraid, consumed by hatred for those who had murdered her father and so many of her friends. But some friends cared enough to pass along the Scriptures and today Sondra's heart is filled with courage, faith, and an incredible love for those whose fury cost her so dearly.

Today, Sondra says that if she sees the man who killed her father, "I will hug him, and tell him Jesus loves him."

Sondra's mother and one of her sisters have also accepted Christ; she is praying that her two other sisters will believe one day, too. Like Nina, they are among the millions who still haven't met Him ... but every day you can tell three youngsters the good news with your commitment of $1 a day as a HOPE GIVER. For more information on this exciting outreach, please call toll-free 1-800-GIV-BIBL (448-2425) or return the coupon in the back of this book with your first month's commitment. It will make an eternal difference to three children in need, every single day.

———

When I was a seven-year-old boy, I received a mandate from the Lord that has charted the course of my life from that moment to the present. It has led me into an ever-increasing scope of ministry until now. We have the possibility of saturating the entire world with the wonderful and never-failing *Truth* - that *Truth* which alone brings *Light* to children sitting in darkness, *Hope* to the hopeless youngsters, *Living Water* to the thirsty little ones, and the *Bread of Hope* to hungry babes. Jesus promised me, "If you will only go, I will go with you. I will show you what you must do."

Now He has placed in our hands the most powerful, most cost-efficient, most effective tool I know of to evangelize the next generation around the world. It takes just 33¢ to reach a child with the *Book of Hope*. We can reach millions every year as we stand together in prayer and faithfulness.

The mandate remains. We must continue to tell youngsters that Jesus loves them and has paid the price for their redemption, that He is coming again, and we must warn them of hell and judgment to come. We must take the Truth of the gospel to them. All they want, all they need is the TRUTH!

A personal message from

BOB HOSKINS

This book was developed out of a deep desire to share with others my compelling sense of urgency to reach the entire world with the gospel message now.

My heart is broken as I travel the world and see the satanic onslaught against the youth and children. Their minds are open; their hearts are ready to respond. If the message of God's love and truth does not reach them, other messages will take hold of their lives.

Book of Hope needs your help to touch these precious ones with the powerful story of Jesus through the *Book of Hope*. Remember, it takes only 33 cents to change a child's life… and in many instances to change an entire family!

Prayerfully consider becoming a *Hope Giver*. That may be a gift of $1.00 a day to reach three children every day of the year, or… God may speak to you to do something entirely different.

If you would like to be a part - write me and let me know how you would like to be involved. I would be delighted to hear from you.

Bob Hoskins

Book of Hope International
3111 SW 10th Street
Pompano, FL 33069
E-mail: info@bookofhope.net
Website: www.hopenet.net

Be a Hope Giver!

You can provide God's Word for 3 children every single day of the year! All it takes is your commitment to pray, and to give $1 a day every day this year. Your gift will be used to provide the *Book of Hope*, our children's Scripture book, for 3 children every day ...

In one year, you'll reach nearly 1,100 children and their families!

Please pray right now about how you can help these children and hundreds more discover the good news of Jesus this year. Then return the Hope Giver coupon below, or send your first monthly gift, marked "Hope Giver" to Book of Hope International. Our address is 3111 SW 10th Street, Pompano, Florida 33069.

Hope Givers

YES, I want to become a HOPE GIVER reaching 3 children with the *Book of Hope* every single day, nearly 1,100 children in one year!

❑   I have enclosed my annual commitment of $365.

❑   I have enclosed my first monthly gift of $31.

❑   Although I cannot become a HOPE GIVER today, I want to help with a special gift of $_____.

NAME_____

ADDRESS_____

CITY, STATE, ZIP_____

Phone _____ E-mail _____

Thank you for your love and generosity.
All gifts are tax-deductible as allowed by law.
Please make checks payable to ***Book of Hope International***.
Our address is 3111 SW 10th Street, Pompano, FL 33069.

BOOK OF HOPE
Exciting video - International Locations -
True-Life Testimonies!

See what God has been doing around the world and how He has changed the destiny of the children and they youth and their families with God's eternal Word.

You can choose the Story of the *Book of Hope*, in which you'll travel with Bob Hoskins to exciting ministry sights!

Or you can select *A Legacy in Eternity* that shows the dramatic impact God's Word has had on the lives of 3 young Russians. It will thrill you as you experience how the *Book of Hope* changed the destiny of these young people, their families and entire communities!

If you choose the *Philippines Special Report* video you will see the powerful story of how God used just two Christian youth to reach some 7,000 college students, and how hundreds were miraculously born again.

FREE VIDEO

Please send my free video:

- ❐ STORY OF THE BOOK OF HOPE
- ❐ A LEGACY IN ETERNITY
- ❐ PHILIPPINES SPECIAL REPORT

Name_____

Address_____

City, State, Zip_____

E-mail _____

Choose your free video - and send $5 for each additional video. Your gift over and above $5 per video will provide the *Book of Hope* for youngsters around the world!

Thank you for your love and generosity. Please make checks payable to *Book of Hope.* Our address is 3111 SW 10th Street, Pompano, Florida, 33069.